Fodor's
Waikiki

New
EDITION

S0-BLN-105

Fodor's Travel Publications, Inc.
New York and London

Grateful acknowledgement is made to Davick Publications for permission to reprint "Diamond Head Inside Out" by Betty Fullard-Leo and "The Aloha Shirt" by DeSoto Brown from *Aloha* Magazine © Davick Publications. Reprinted with permission from Davick Publications.

Fodor's Waikiki

Editor: Jillian Magalaner
Editorial Contributors: Jim Ariyoshi, Rita Ariyoshi, Carmen Anthony, Michael Flynn, Anita Guerrini, Julia Lisella, Marty Wentzel
Art Director: Fabrizio La Rocca
Cartographer: David Lindroth
Illustrator: Karl Tanner
Cover Photograph: Kishimoto/Uniphoto

Design: Vignelli Associates

Special Sales

Contents

Foreword

We wish to express our gratitude to Nancy Daniels and Tom Herman for their assistance in the preparation of this guidebook.

While every care has been taken to ensure the accuracy of the information in this guide, the passage of time will always bring change, and consequently, the publisher cannot accept responsibility for errors that may occur.

All prices and opening times quoted here are based on information supplied to us at press time. Hours and admission fees may change, however, and the prudent traveler will avoid inconvenience by calling ahead.

Fodor's wants to hear about your travel experiences, both pleasant and unpleasant. When a hotel or restaurant fails to live up to its billing, let us know and we will investigate the complaint and revise our entries where the facts warrant it.

Send your letters to the editors of Fodor's Travel Publications, 201 E. 50th Street, New York, NY 10022.

Highlights'92 and Fodor's Choice

Highlights '92

Waikiki has never looked better. The resort's massive multimillion-dollar renovation has refurbished the area from top to bottom. The saw-horses, jackhammers, and construction detours are gone, and so is the accompanying noise and confusion. Waikiki has once again assumed its throne as the queen of tropical resorts.

Along the main street. More than $10.5 million dollars has brought a new look to Kalakaua Avenue, making the famous main street that parallels the beach a grand thoroughfare. Sidewalks have been widened, traffic realigned, street signs improved, and clutter removed. Underfoot, earthtone tiles in tapa-like Polynesian designs pave the sidewalks. Kiosks, benches, stately coconut palms, flowers, and festive night lighting all make Kalakaua Avenue a great place for strolling, day or night. New shops with well-known names add so much glitz and glamour that parts of Hawaii's most famous avenue are beginning to look like Rodeo Drive in Beverly Hills. **Tiffany, Hermès, Chanel, Celine,** and **Gucci** are bringing designer chic to the land of grass skirts and flower leis.

The oldest hotel in town. The historic restoration of Waikiki's oldest hotel, the **Moana,** now called the **Sheraton Moana Surfrider,** is completed. The elegant Victorian grande dame of hotels, built in 1901, now looks like a magnificent wedding cake among the modern towers. There were very few compromises made in the Moana's restoration; Sheraton is to be commended for spending the money and going all the way with this one.

Sitting on the Moana's wide veranda during afternoon high tea, with a sandalwood fan (provided by the hotel), sipping something tall and cool with a wedge of pineapple on the glass rim, and listening to classical music while the tide rolls in is an experience to remember, a quiet moment packed with nostalgia for restful, more gracious days. In the morning, breakfast is served on the veranda, and there isn't a nicer spot in town. Sunday brunch is now served in the oceanside Grand Salon, and Hawaiiana programs are presented beneath the spreading boughs of the huge banyan tree, where Robert Louis Stevenson once composed stories for the beautiful young Princess Kaiulani.

The hotel's Historical Room, in the rotunda overlooking the main entrance, displays old photographs, dance cards, menus (note the prices and weep), dishes, silverware, and other fascinating memorabilia, most of them sent to the Moana by former guests.

The room, the porches, and veranda are all open to the public and draw a steady crowd of local people hoping to recapture the Hawaii of a bygone era.

Waikiki's newest hotel. First it was supposed to open in 1989 and they were calling it the Waikiki Prince. Now open and welcoming guests, Waikiki's newest hotel is known as the **Hawaii Prince Hotel.** With 521 rooms in two tall towers, this may very well be Waikiki's last big hotel, because the resort has simply run out of room. Built at a cost of $150 million, the luxury property overlooks the Ala Wai Yacht Harbor and offers five restaurants and a grand ballroom. The restaurants provide a very welcome addition to Waikiki's inventory of fine dining establishments. Included in the five are the hotel's signature dining room, the Prince Court, and the Hakone, a copy of the Maui Prince's classic Kyoto-style Japanese restaurant.

The whaling wall goes extinct. The 20-story mural painted on the side of the Waikiki Marina condominium, right at the entrance to Waikiki, is almost totally obscured by the Hawaii Prince Hotel. The last of the great humpbacks now swims behind the hotel wall, although sections of the half-acre mural, showing whales and other marine life, can still be seen from the lodging's deck area and near the front entrance.

The biggest resort on the island. About $100 million has already been spent on the **Hilton Hawaiian Village** for renovations and additions, and they're still spending and adding. The latest word is that the hotel will be developing a complete health-spa complex including tennis courts and a gourmet health-food restaurant.

The Golden Dragon, the Village's premier Chinese restaurant, has moved to the Rainbow Tower overlooking the lagoon, and has a romantic outdoor dining area. In addition to serving the best Chinese food in Honolulu, with such dishes as Imperial Beggar's Chicken (wrapped in lotus leaves and baked in clay, and requiring 24 hours' notice), the restaurant has a restrained and sophisticated decor radiating a serene, Asian ambience. The serving staff includes Sylon the Tea Lady, star of a little tea drama enacted at each table. She also tells fortunes at no extra charge.

More Village entertainment. It's one of the best pageants in Waikiki, and it's free. Every Friday evening the Hilton Hawaiian Village stages its King Kalakaua Jubilee, poolside, with the beach as a backdrop. It's a monarchy-era musical presentation with pomp, song, hula, a fire swallower, and painless history, culminating in a spectacular fireworks show.

Waikiki's biggest name dinner show. This one's at the Hilton Hawaiian Village, too. Charo, the coochie-coochie girl, is wowing them at the hotel's Tropic's Surf Club. If you add up her years in show business, it would indicate that Charo is

no spring chicken, but she still has the face and body of a
teenybopper and she prances her way through a high-ener-
gy salsa performance in drop-dead costumes. The buffet
dinner is pretty good, too. Charo joins Hilton's star lineup
consisting of the legendary Don Ho and his Polynesian ex-
travaganza at the Village Dome Showroom, jazzman Jimmy
Borges playing Gershwin, Cole Porter, and Jerome Kern
dance tunes in the Paradise Lounge, and a host of other top
Hawaiian entertainers at the hotel's various bars and
lounges.

Sushi in Surferland. Located on the North Shore of Oahu
(legendary for its winter waves and championship surfing
competitions) the Turtle Bay Hilton has introduced the are-
a's first Japanese restaurant, **Asahi.** Select from 50 kinds of
sushi, or choose tempura or teriyaki. The hotel has also just
expanded its Sunday brunch to include a waffle bar and taco
bar. The floor-to-ceiling windows in the Sea Tide Room look
out on surfers riding those fabulous waves.

Book a boutique. Mega-resorts may be the mega-trend, but
small boutique hotels are continuing to spring up in Waikiki, offering intimate, personalized alternatives. First, in
1988, came the **Waikiki Joy,** placing an emphasis on high-
tech amenities, followed by the **Coconut Plaza** with its chic
decor and low rates. At press time, Aston Hotels & Resorts
has plans to open the refurbished **Aston Waikiki Beachside,**
an Island boutique hotel with a decidedly European flair.

A sinking feeling. Atlantis Submarines, operating for years
in the Caribbean, now has a 65-foot, 80-ton sub going down
off Waikiki. It carries up to 46 passengers in comfortable
seats, each facing a big viewing porthole, and dives to a
depth of 100 feet. This is a real sub that really dives, not a
Disney thrill ride. The Atlantis people, working in coopera-
tion with the University of Hawaii, have sunk a 174-foot
ship, constructed an artificial reef at the dive site, and plan
to sink an airplane. The underwater attractions have drawn
schools of colorful reef fish which are fed leftovers from the
Hilton's champagne breakfast by Atlantis scuba divers. It's
quite a sight. The really sad aspect of the experience is the
knowledge that the fish that were once so naturally bounti-
ful in the area have been depleted by the foreign drift-net
fishermen operating in Hawaiian waters in the past few
years. The ocean floor just feet away from the feeding sight
is a desert. Included in the Atlantis dive fee is a catamaran
ride to the dive site, and a sailing tour of the Waikiki and
Diamond Head shoreline.

A new high. Aloha IslandAir, the commuter arm of the
interisland giant, **Aloha Airlines,** has initiated one-day
flightseeing tours of Oahu, Molokai, Lanai, Maui, Kahoola-
we, and the Big Island aboard a specially equipped de
Havilland Dash-6 aircraft with excellent viewing windows
and individual headsets. The tour includes Hawaii Volcanoes National Park, on the Big Island; Maui's Haleakala

Crater; a visit to the 225,000-acre Parker Ranch, the largest privately owned ranch in the United States, located on the Big Island; a 2½-hour stop in Lahaina, Maui's historical whaling town; and a visit to Kalaupapa Peninsula on Molokai, where Father Damien labored among the victims of Hansen's disease (leprosy). The site, at the foot of Molokai's sea cliffs, which are the tallest in the world, is now an incredibly beautiful and emotionally moving national park. The tour departs daily from Honolulu and includes pickup in Waikiki, lunch in Lahaina, and a color photograph.

A big new resort on Oahu. The sunny forecast for Hawaii's tourism industry and lack of room for expansion in Waikiki have encouraged the construction of **Ko Olina,** a vast $3 billion resort along the dry Ewa Coast west of Honolulu International Airport. It will include seven hotels having a total of 4,000 rooms, 5,200 condominium units, a 44-acre marina, its own 18-hole golf course, a tennis complex, and a shopping center. Situated on 642 acres, it will be the state's largest resort. Some 3,000 coconut palms have already been planted. Among the hotels now under construction or planned are the **Pan Pacific, Loew's,** and the **Four Seasons.** A luxury seaside condo named the **Royal Ko Olina** will have 320 luxury units complete with limousine and pantry services and a health club.

A whole new city on Oahu. Also slated for the West Beach area is a "second city" to absorb Hawaii's phenomenal growth. It will have single-family homes, condominiums, and a business district.

Cheering up Chinatown. The area had long languished in the shadow of Honolulu's downtown skyscrapers, almost forgotten, pursuing its fragrant (the smells of incense, fish, and flowers mingling), mysterious lifestyle, slightly tawdry, a little rickety, but always fascinating. Now a renaissance has drawn artists, smart galleries, and little restaurants to the area where they reside among the lei stands, noodle shops, and herbalists. It's suddenly chic to have a shop in Chinatown.

Food news. Led by a bright, young group of talented European and American chefs, Hawaii is developing its own distinctive regional cuisine, using the area's unique produce and combining aspects of classical French and California nouvelle with the traditional cooking styles of Asia. After several attempts at naming the trend, foodies seem to have adopted "Pacific Rim Cuisine" as the most descriptive term. The new cuisine has been earning national attention, and some of the best places to sample it are right in Waikiki.

Getting off the ground. Because of the vagaries of airport construction, the **Pacific Aerospace Museum,** which is said to have cost $2 million, still has not opened at Honolulu International Airport. When it is finally launched (no firm date was set at press time), it will have a multimedia theater which will allow visitors to stand seemingly on the deck of a space shuttle, witness the infamous attack on Pearl Harbor, and fly into the airport itself.

The Convention Center controversy continues. Honolulu has needed a major convention facility for a long time. The big question has been where to put it. In its 1988 session, the Hawaii State Legislature chose the International Market Place as the site, leaving many segments of the travel industry aghast at the decision to place the convention center in the heart of already crowded Waikiki—and wipe out a popular tourist attraction at the same time. The options are still open, however, because another site just outside Waikiki near Ala Moana Shopping Center, has just been approved for development by First Development, Inc., of Tokyo. The complex will include a 500-foot hotel tower and two 450-foot condominium towers. They will be Hawaii's tallest buildings. Provided the project doesn't run into government snags, Honolulu may end up with two convention centers: The Tokyo-financed International Market Place, slated to cost over a billion dollars, should be completed sometime in 1994.

Sighs of the times. The Kodak Hula Show, which has offered free performances in Waikiki for 50 years, is now charging an admission fee of $2.50. A Kodak spokesman said the charge is necessary to defray mounting costs; any profits will be donated to charity.

For kids of all ages. The new Hawaii Children's Museum has opened in the revamped Dole Pineapple Cannery, renamed Dole Cannery Square. The focus of the museum is "You, the Child." The hands-on displays include a bicycle-riding skeleton, and a huge mouth which allows the little ones to climb inside for a different view of what proper brushing is all about.

Fodor's Choice

No two people will agree on what makes a perfect vacation, but it's fun and helpful to know what others think. We hope you'll have a chance to experience some of Fodor's Choices yourself while visiting Waikiki. For detailed information about each entry, refer to the appropriate chapters in this guidebook.

Beaches

Bellows Beach on the weekends

Kailua Beach

Sans Souci Beach

Waikiki in front of the Hyatt Regency Hotel

Waikiki in front of the Royal Hawaiian Hotel

Waimea Bay in summer (the surf can be extremely dangerous in winter)

Best Buys

Aloha shirts—Andrade for quality; outlets and street stalls for price

Ethnic finds—Mandalay, Kitamura's

Fine jewelry—Haimoff & Haimoff

Funky fashion—Chocolates for Breakfast for women, Altillo for men

Hawaiian arts and crafts—Little Hawaiian Craft Shop

Most fun—Shirokiya

Muumuus—Liberty House stores

Variety—Ala Moana Shopping Center

Drives

From Hawaii Kai to Waimanalo

Likelike Highway on the windward side

Pali Highway

Festivals

Aloha Week Festival

Kamehameha Day

Lei Day

For Kids

Honolulu Zoo, especially the giraffe tower

Oceanarium Restaurant, Pacific Beach Hotel

Sea Life Park

Surfing lessons, Waikiki Beach

Waikiki Aquarium

Golf Courses

Olomana Golf Links, public

Waialae Country Club, if you know a member

Hotels

Colony Surf *(Very Expensive)*

Halekulani *(Very Expensive)*

Hyatt Regency Waikiki *(Very Expensive)*

Kahala Hilton *(Very Expensive)*

Royal Hawaiian *(Very Expensive)*

Hilton Hawaiian Village *(Expensive)*

Waikiki Joy *(Expensive)*

Coconut Plaza *(Moderate)*

Waikikian on the Beach *(Moderate)*

Kamaaina (Islanders') Favorites

Manapua (a steamed bun with sweet pork filling) from any lunch wagon at Sandy Beach

Poi lunch at The Willows

Shave ice with vanilla ice cream and *azuki* beans at Aoki's in Haleiwa

Sunday brunch at the Halekulani

Sunset picnic at Queen's Beach

Luau

Royal Hawaiian Hotel

Local Dishes

Any local seafood, especially opakapaka

Laulau

Lomilomi salmon

Macadamia nut cream pie at the Willows

Manapua

Mango anything, in season

Passion-orange juice

"Plate lunch" from one of the beach lunch wagons—not gourmet, but an experience

Poha jam

Saimin (noodle soup that might include shrimp, green onion, fish cake, and pork)

Nightlife

The Black Orchid

Danny Kaleikini Show, Kahala Hilton

Nicholas Nickolas

Nick's Fishmarket

Polynesian Cultural Center Evening Show

Trappers, Hyatt Regency Waikiki

Restaurants

Kamaaina Suite, The Willows *(Very Expensive)*

La Mer, Halekulani Hotel *(Very Expensive)*

Best Japanese—Kacho, Waikiki Parc Hotel *(Expensive)*

Best Seafood—Nick's Fishmarket *(Expensive)*

Baci *(Moderate)*

Best Chinese—Golden Dragon, Hilton Hawaiian Village *(Moderate)*

Bon Appetit *(Moderate)*

Orchids, Halekulani Hotel *(Moderate)*

Romantic Hideaways

Breakfast at Michel's at the Colony Surf

Dinner at The Secret

Lunch at the Tahitian Lanai

Picnic at the Waikiki Shell

Room in the old section of the Royal Hawaiian Hotel

Sights

Arizona Memorial

Byodo-In Temple

Polynesian Cultural Center

Sea Life Park

Sunsets

Diamond Head Lighthouse

Sunset Beach, North Shore

Waikiki Beach

Views

Makapuu Point

Nuuanu Pali Lookout

Top of the Ilikai Waikiki Hotel

Upper ocean-view rooms at the Sheraton Waikiki and Halekulani hotels

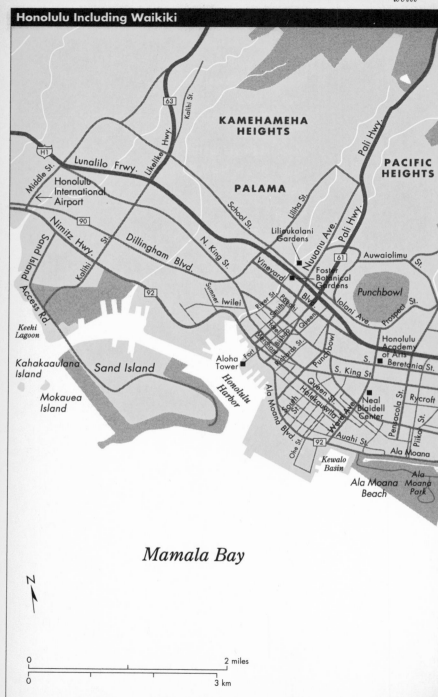

Honolulu Including Waikiki

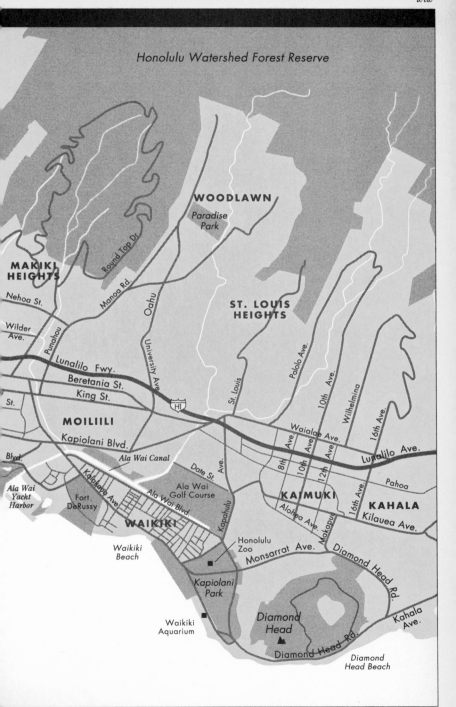

Honolulu Watershed Forest Reserve

WOODLAWN

Paradise Park

MAKIKI HEIGHTS

Round Top Dr.

Manoa Rd.

Oahu

University Ave.

ST. LOUIS HEIGHTS

Nehoa St.

Wilder Ave.

Punahou

Lunalilo Fwy.

Beretania St.

King St.

St.

St. Louis

H1

Palolo Ave.

10th Ave.

Wilhelmina

16th Ave.

MOILIILI

Kapiolani Blvd.

Waialae Ave.

8th Ave.

10th Ave.

12th Ave.

Lunalilo Ave.

Blvd.

Ala Wai Canal

Date St.

Ave.

Pahoa

Ala Wai Yacht Harbor

Kalakaua Ave.

Fort DeRussy

Ala Wai Blvd.

Ala Wai Golf Course

Kapahulu

KAIMUKI

Alohea Ave.

Makapuu

16th Ave.

KAHALA

Kilauea Ave.

WAIKIKI

Waikiki Beach

Honolulu Zoo

Monsarrat Ave.

Diamond Head Rd.

Kapiolani Park

Waikiki Aquarium

Diamond Head ▲

Diamond Head Rd.

Kahala Ave.

Diamond Head Rd.

Diamond Head Beach

World Time Zones

MONDAY
SUNDAY

International Date Line

+12 +13 -9 -4 -3

-10 -7 -5 -4

-11 -8 -6

-10

+11

+12

Numbers below vertical bands relate each zone to Greenwich Mean Time (0 hrs.).
Local times frequently differ from these general indications,
as indicated by light-face numbers on map.

+11   +12 -   -11   -10   -9   -8   -7   -6   -5   -4   -3   -2

Algiers, **29**   Berlin, **34**   Delhi, **48**   Istanbul, **40**
Anchorage, **3**   Bogotá, **19**   Denver, **8**   Jerusalem, **42**
Athens, **41**   Budapest, **37**   Djakarta, **53**   Johannesburg, **44**
Auckland, **1**   Buenos Aires, **24**   Dublin, **26**   Lima, **20**
Baghdad, **46**   Caracas, **22**   Edmonton, **7**   Lisbon, **28**
Bangkok, **50**   Chicago, **9**   Hong Kong, **56**   London (Greenwich), **27**
Beijing, **54**   Copenhagen, **33**   Honolulu, **2**   Los Angeles, **6**
                        Dallas, **10**   Madrid, **38**
                                                                        Manila, **57**

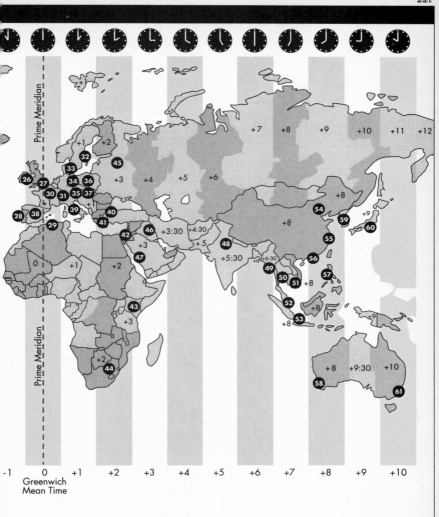

-1 0 +1 +2 +3 +4 +5 +6 +7 +8 +9 +10
Greenwich
Mean Time

Introduction

Waikiki—the very word conjures images as diverse as dreams. Some people think of a full moon seeming to rest atop majestic Diamond Head, while silver-crested waves sweep toward a sandy shore. For others, Waikiki is Surf City—free, easy, and loud, a youth hangout in Paradise. Television fans recall Jack Lord on *Hawaii Five-O* snapping, "Book 'em, Dano," or the more recent *Magnum, P.I.'s* Tom Selleck racing down the main drag of Kalakaua Avenue in his red Ferrari. And let's face it, for some people, Waikiki brings to mind a tacky tourist trap bursting with more than 4 million annual visitors. Each of these visions has a ring of truth to it, but the eclectic destination is not so easily categorized.

Hawaii's most famous resort has long been considered "holiday central" for kings and commoners alike. King Kalakaua kept a boat house here. The lovely Princess Kaiulani had a home along its sun-washed shores. It was here that Robert Louis Stevenson penned his memorable poetry and prose beneath a spreading banyan tree, Amelia Earhart took rest from her adventures, and the Prince of Wales (later Edward VII) danced beneath the stars.

Almost a hundred years later, Waikiki has come of age. It is no longer a languid tropical outpost, but a sophisticated resort city on the order of Rio de Janeiro or Hong Kong. Sure, the scenery is just as lovely, the sunsets are sheer poetry, the ocean is clear, the air is pure, and the food is better than ever. But Waikiki has stepped up the pace.

Waikiki has more action packed within its perimeters than all the rest of Hawaii combined. Bordered by the ocean on the south, it sparkles along 2½ miles of spangled sea from the famous Diamond Head landmark on the east to the Ala Wai Yacht Harbor on the west. Separated from the sprawling city of Honolulu by the broad Ala Wai Canal on its northern boundary, Waikiki is 3½ miles from downtown Honolulu and worlds apart from any other city in the world. Nowhere else is there such a salad of cultures so artfully tossed, each one retaining its distinct flavor and texture. McDonald's offers burgers and *saimin*, the ubiquitous noodle soup of Nippon. You'll find yourself saying things like *aloha* and *mahalo* (thank you). You'll come across almost as many sushi bars as ice cream stands.

Hundreds of thousands of visitors now sleep in the more than 34,000 rooms of Waikiki's nearly 175 hotels and condominiums. To this 1.5-square-mile Pacific playground come sun bunnies, honeymooners, Marines on holiday, long-staying Europeans, Canadians, and Japanese, and every other type of tourist imaginable. Waikiki vibrates with international excitement and offers more to see, do, and eat than all the other Hawaiian islands combined.

Take the nightlife. If you were a mega star, wouldn't you want to book a few days in Hawaii on your world tour? Most do. There's also a good crop of local talent, ranging from the old pro Don Ho and his Vegas-style hula show to luaus on the beach, video discos, and old-fashioned cheek-to-cheek dancing beneath the palms at the Royal Hawaiian Hotel. The cabarets keep the nightlife going till 4 AM.

Hawaii is the cultural and commercial crossroads of the Pacific, and Waikiki is its economic base. Waikiki is where most of Hawaii's more than 6 million annual visitors spend at least a few nights. Because of these factors, the shops in Waikiki are bursting with the wares of the world, everything from Australian sheepskins to Oriental jade to Paris designer fashions. You can choose between a vulgar ashtray or a magnificent handcrafted rug from mainland China. Women can outfit themselves in a basic black Chanel dress or a neon-orange muumuu, while the men can pick a brazen aloha shirt or an imported Mondo Tallia suit. In between the two extremes, beautifully made resort wear is setting the pace in the lucrative world of fashion.

Dining has come to be one of the great Waikiki experiences. The area's chefs and restaurateurs, particularly in the large hotels and a variety of independent dining spots, share a commitment to excellence. Waikiki boasts some of the Aloha State's best meals. You'll find cordon bleu chefs, and veterans of Maxim's in Paris and the Four Seasons in New York. These practioners of what's been dubbed "Pacific Rim Cuisine" now whip up wok dishes with a French flair, wrapping taro and local lobster in phyllo pastry, and create new culinary delights with passion fruit. Of course, there's still meat and potatoes, fish, and poi aplenty, along with a bounty of moderately priced restaurants and a glut of snack bars, budget eateries, all-you-can-eat buffets, and brand-name burgers. To spice the pot, there's Thai, Greek, Korean, Indian, French, German, Mexican, and Italian food. In all, the restaurants number nearly 250 in Waikiki alone.

Even with all these attractions, the star of Waikiki is still the beach—that 2½-mile strand of golden sand, anchored by familiar Diamond Head on one end and melting into golden sunsets beyond the Ala Wai Yacht Harbor on the other. Fringed by palms and festooned with glittering hotels, it is easily one of the best swimming beaches in the world, gentle with a sandy bottom, clean and sparkling.

Waikiki has a special quality to it that sets it apart from other places. Couples who probably haven't held hands in 20 years touch tenderly like schoolchildren—there he is in his brown shoes and walking shorts and she with a flower in her gray hair. Honeymooners from Japan laugh shyly, playing in the surf, and servicemen clown on aqua bikes. There's the glory of a first surfing lesson, when you actually stand up and ride a wave, girls with their hair streaming behind them and grins lighting their faces, boys affecting a casual stance—the California hot-dawg look. Everyone is having fun.

Most of Hawaii's visitors have been here before. That says a lot when there are other sunny places in the world, and many are a lot closer to home and cheaper.

One of the impressive things about Waikiki is the manner in which people are treated. We've all traveled, and we know the difference between being treated well and being treated rudely. And let's face it, we often judge a whole country, a whole group of people, by the actions of a few. Let a taxi driver snap at us—and we won't return. Let one man go out of his way to show us the right road, and we wax euphoric about how friendly and warm the people are.

Whether it's the stark realization that tourism is Hawaii's number one business, accounting for one out of every three dollars of the state's revenue, or whether it's the Hawaiian tradition of hospitality, the visitor is king. He or she is treated with kindness and welcomed with a sincere warmth. The welcome is part good business and part the real spirit of aloha that still pervades every aspect of Hawaiian life. It's this spirit, as much as the postcard beauty of the place, that sets Waikiki apart.

Waikiki is only one glittering part of the cosmopolitan city of Honolulu, America's only city with a royal past. The business pace is brisk, yet the people flit among the skyscrapers in flowing muumuus and bright aloha shirts. The scene includes tree-shaded parks, temples that look like they were transported intact from the Orient, and impressive examples of the arts, from opera and French impressionist paintings to kabuki and the Japanese tea ceremony.

The residents live in towering condominiums in the suburbs or in little white houses tucked deep in the valleys. There are no slums, although portions of downtown look like a seedy, tattered seaport catering to the fleets of the world. The wonderful old buildings of the area are beginning to attract artists and gallery owners and a few good restaurateurs who are willing to brave the tawdriness in exchange for great space at low rent. They ignite the blighted blocks with smart mauve-and-alabaster-tone windows.

With the cost of living here being the second highest in the nation, most Honolulu men and women work. These workers eat at more fast-food restaurants per capita than in most places and are subjected to choked freeways during rush hour. Still, most Honolulans wouldn't trade their city for any other. Most of them can be at the beach in minutes, and going out for an evening of dinner and the theater is not a major project. The distances are manageable.

Honolulu is located on the island of Oahu, which encompasses only 608 square miles. Third largest of the Hawaiian Islands, Oahu was formed by two volcanoes that erupted 4 million to 6 million years ago and eventually created a peaceable kingdom of 608 square miles. More than 80% of Hawaii's one million residents live on Oahu, yet somehow there is enough room for wide-open spaces and sufficient time to take a deep breath and relax.

More and more Hawaiians are stepping forward to say that Oahu is their favorite island, and many claim that is has the most spectacular scenery of all Hawaii. Part of its dramatic appearance can be attributed to its majestic highlands: the western Waianae Mountains, which rise 4,000 feet above sea level, and the verdant Koolaus, which cross the island's midsection at elevations of more than 3,000 feet. After eons of erosion by wind and weather, these ranges now have sculptured, jagged peaks, deep valleys, sheer green cliffs, and dynamic vistas. Below the mountains, Oahu is a gathering place of beach parks, with more than 50 draped around its edges like a beautiful lei. Many of the parks include restrooms, showers, and picnic tables sprinkled along the shoreline. Each beach is known for a different ocean activity, such as snorkeling, bodysurfing, swimming, or windsurfing.

The center of the island is carpeted in pineapple plantations. Acres of waving sugarcane go down almost to the sea. There are ranches, banana farms, and fields of exotic flowers grown for export. The plantation towns are small. Some have become cute with boutiques and little art galleries. Others are just themselves—old, wooden, and picturesque—the small homes surrounded by a riot of flowers and trees heavy with mango, pomelo, and lychee.

Hawaii's kings and queens ruled from Honolulu's Iolani Palace, near the present downtown. It was at Iolani that the American flag first flew over the Islands. Even in those days of royalty, the virtues of Waikiki as a playground were noticed. Long processions of *alii* (nobility) would make their way across the streams and swamps, past the duck ponds, to the coconut groves and the beach.

By the 1880s, guest houses were sprinkled along the beach like confetti. The first hotel, the Moana (now the refurbished Sheraton Moana Surfrider), was built at the turn of the century. At that time, Waikiki was connected to the rest of Honolulu by a tram, bringing townspeople to the shore. In 1927, the "Pink Palace of the Pacific," the Royal Hawaiian Hotel, was built by Matson Navigation Company to accommodate travelers arriving on luxury liners. It was opened with a grand ball, and Waikiki was launched as a first-class tourist destination, duck ponds, taro patches, and all. The rich and famous came from around the world. December 7, 1941, brought that era to a close, with the bombing of Pearl Harbor and Hawaii's entry into the war in the Pacific. The Royal Hawaiian was turned over to American servicemen. Hundreds of war-weary soldiers and sailors found a warm welcome in Waikiki.

With victory came the boom. By 1952, Waikiki had 2,000 hotel rooms. In 1969, there were 15,000 rooms. Today, that figure has more than doubled.

Waikiki sits on the sunny dry side of Oahu, one of the eight major Hawaiian islands, seven of which are inhabited. In all, there are 132 Hawaiian isles and atolls, stretched across 1,600 miles of ocean. Hawaii is America's most exotic, most unusual state, and Waikiki is its generator, keeping everything humming. It incorporates all the natural splendors of the Islands and synthesizes them with elegance and daring into an international resort city in the middle of the vast blue Pacific.

1 Essential Information

Before You Go

Visitor Information

A trip is a considerable investment of both time and money, and it's hard to say which is more precious these days. A travel agent who has been to Hawaii can help you cut through a lot of the details. He or she will also know most of the airline packages and special tours, and these can represent significant savings.

Most travel agents work on a commission from the airlines, hotels, and attractions. You pay no more—and often less—than if you made your arrangements on your own.

The source of all information on Hawaii is the **Hawaii Visitors Bureau** (HVB). The bureau's main office is located right in Waikiki (2270 Kalakaua Ave., 8th floor, Honolulu, 96815, tel. 808/923–1811).

HVB is a sophisticated communications network attuned to the needs of the visitor, and consumer oriented. The bureau publishes three free booklets. The *Calendar of Events* lists all the special holidays and annual festivals. Just give the staff your arrival date and they'll mail the appropriate booklet. The bureau also publishes an *Accommodation Guide*, which lists the various lodging choices in Hawaii in every price range. The guide tells you how close an accommodation is to the beach, and whether it has a pool and such amenities as refrigerators and televisions. The third is a *Restaurant Guide,* listing the more than 500 HVB-member restaurants in the state, each with a one-line description and a price category. There are no rating systems in the guides, just the bare facts.

The bureau also maintains offices on the Mainland:

New York: 441 Lexington Ave., Room 1407, NY 10017, tel. 212/986–9203.
Los Angeles: 3440 Wilshire Blvd., CA 90010, tel. 213/385–5301.
Chicago: 180 N. Michigan Ave., Suite 1031, IL 60601, tel. 312/236–0632.
San Francisco: 50 California St., CA 94111, tel. 415/392–8173.

HVB Meetings and Conventions office:

Washington, DC: 1511 K St. NW, Suite 415, DC 20005, tel. 202/393–6752.

Regional offices:

Canada: 4915 Cedar Crescent, Delta, B.C., Canada, V4M 1J9, tel. 604/943–8555.
Great Britain: 2 Cinnamon Row, Plantation Wharf, York Pl., London SW11 3TW, tel. 071/924–3999.
Japan: 129 Kokusai Bldg., 1–1, 3-chome, Maruno-uchi, Chiyoda-ku, Tokyo, Japan 100, tel. 03/287–2651 or 2652.

Tour Groups

Like most things in the Islands, package tours are a bit more laid-back than in other parts of the world. They usually include airfare, accommodations, transfers, some sightseeing, and plenty of free time to put some sand between your toes. Choosing a tour often comes down to how inclusive you want it to be:

Do you want to know all your meals are paid for before you leave, or would you rather hunt out the local eatery? Would you prefer to arrange a private sail, or is a group outing on a catamaran fine with you? Both preferences are easily accommodated.

When considering a tour, be sure to find out exactly what expenses are included (particularly tips, taxes, side trips, additional meals, and entertainment), ratings of all hotels on the itinerary and the facilities they offer, cancellation policies for both you and the tour operator, and the cost of the single supplement if you are traveling alone. Most tour operators request that bookings be made through a travel agent; there is no additional charge for doing so.

General-Interest Tours
Maupintour (Box 807, Lawrence, KA 66044, tel. 913/843–1211 or 800/255–4266) offers tours to Oahu teamed with the other islands. A 13-day trip to all four islands includes helicopter "flightseeing." **American Express Vacations** (Box 5014, Atlanta, GA 30302, tel. 800/241–1700 or in Georgia, 800/282–0800) is a veritable supermarket of tours. **Pleasant Hawaiian Holidays** (2404 Townsgate Rd., Box 5020, Westlake Village, CA 91359, tel. 818/991–3390 or 800/242–9244) also offers tours by the cartful, including low-priced packages for short visits. **Talmage Tours** (1223 Walnut St., Philadelphia, PA 19107, tel. 215/923–7100) has a nine-day Waikiki and Kauai package. Other major operators include **Cartan Tours** (12755 Hwy. 55, Suite 101, Minneapolis, MN 55441, tel. 612/540–8999) and **Tauck Tours** (11 Wilton Rd., Westport, CT 06881, tel. 203/226–6911 or 800/468–2825).

British Tour Operators
Albany Travel (Manchester) Ltd. Central Bldgs., 211 Deansgate, Manchester M2 5QR, tel. 061/83–0202) offers packages of seven nights or more, with an option to combine stays on several islands.

Hawaiian Holidays Tours, Inc. (10 Hill St., Richmond, Surrey TW9 1TN, tel. 081/948–3535), is the only Hawaiian company directly available to the European market, and all its prices are quoted in dollars. It offers self-drive or sightseeing packages to the five main islands, with stays in hotels or condominiums. It also offers escorted tours to Oahu, the Big Island, Maui, and Kauai. Round-trip airfares from London to Honolulu are *not* included.

Jetsave (Sussex House, London Rd., East Grinstead, West Sussex RH19 1LD, tel. 0342/312033) offers seven nights at Waikiki Beach and the "Hawaiian Medley" air tour which combines a week in Hawaii with stays in Los Angeles and San Francisco.

Poundstretcher (Airlink House, Hazlewick Ave., Three Bridges, Crawley, West Sussex RH10 1YS, tel. 0293/518022) offers hotel vacations for seven nights from £685, or at a holiday village with prices for seven nights from £835 and 14 nights from £1,099. It also offers two other vacations: Waikiki and Maui for 14 nights from £899 or Waikiki and Kauai for 14 nights from £965.

Package Deals for Independent Travelers

Gogo Tours (69 Spring St., Ramsey, NJ 07446, tel. 201/934–3500 or 800/821–3731) has packages ranging from 2 to 16 days with options for sightseeing and discounted car rental. **American Express**'s 50-page Hawaii brochure has a wide selection of independent packages. **Classic Hawaii** (65 W. Santa Clara St., San Jose, CA 95113, tel. 405/287–9101 or 800/221–3949) has packages featuring upscale hotels and resorts. Also check with **Delta Airlines** (tel. 800/872–7786 or 404/765–2952), **United Airlines** (tel. 800/328–6877 or 312/952–4000), **TWA Getaway Vacations** (tel. 800/GET–AWAY), **American Fly AAway Vacations** (tel. 800/433–7300 or 817/355–1234), and **Continental Airlines** (tel. 713/821–2100).

Passports, Visas, and Customs

Travel Documents Persons who are not citizens of the United States require a passport and a visa. Canadians only need to prove their place of birth with a passport, birth certificate, or similar document. British travelers will need a valid, 10-year passport (cost £15) and a U.S. Visitor's Visa, which you can get either through your travel agent or by post from the **United States Embassy, Visa and Immigration Dept.** (5 Upper Grosvenor St., London W1A 2JB, tel. 071/499–3443 recorded message, or 499–7010). The embassy no longer accepts visa applications made by personal callers. No vaccinations are required.

Restrictions on Import and Export Plants and plant products are subject to control by the Department of Agriculture, both on entering and leaving Hawaii. Pineapples and coconuts pass freely; papayas must be treated. All other fruits are banned for export to the U.S. mainland. Flowers pass except for gardenia, rose leaves, jade vine, and mauna loa. Seeds, except in leis and jewelry, are banned. Also banned are insects, snails, coffee, cotton, cacti, sugarcane, all berries, and soil.

Customs for British Travelers If you are 21 or over, you may take in 200 cigarettes or 50 cigars or two kilograms of tobacco; one liter of alcohol; and duty-free gifts to a value of $100. Be careful not to try to take in meat or meat products, seeds, plants, or fruits. Avoid illegal drugs like the plague.

Returning to the United Kingdom, you may take home, if you are 17 and over: (1) 200 cigarettes or 100 cigarillos or 50 cigars or 250 grams of tobacco; (2) two liters of table wine and (a) one liter of alcohol over 22% by volume (most spirits), or (b) two liters of alcohol under 22% by volume (fortified or sparkling wine), (3) 60 milliliters of perfume and ¼ liter of toilet water; and (4) other goods up to a value of £32.

Pets Leave dogs and other pets at home. A strict 120-day quarantine is imposed to keep out rabies, which is nonexistent in Hawaii. For full details, write to the **Animal Quarantine Station, Department of Agriculture,** State of Hawaii, 99–770 Moanalua Rd., Aiea, HI 96701.

When to Go

Hawaii has been called the land of eternal June. Blessed with sunshine and cooled by trade winds, it has one of the most ideal climates in the world. Situated well within the tropics, at latitude 20, Waikiki's year-round temperatures are mild, with a comfortable average of 75–80 degrees F (23–25 degrees C). The tropical location also means that there's little variation in the amount of daylight whether in June or December. The shortest day is 11 hours and the longest, 13½. When day finally surrenders to night, the sun goes down off Waikiki in a blaze of glory, painting the sky and ocean in passionate vermilion, scarlet, and gold. A fleet of pleasure boats waits to take you out to sea on sunset cruises with music and dancing. It's even more dramatic watching from the sand, as the sun silhouettes the volcanic Waianae Mountains and the surfers ride waves tinged with gold.

With such a consistently good climate, Waikiki's peak tourist seasons have more to do with the weather elsewhere. Pale hordes with parkas over their arms arrive in mid-December, and the crowds don't thin until April. Room rates run 10%–15% higher during this period than during the rest of the year. Summer, during the school vacation, is another crowded time for Waikiki, when families and young people gather, but the rates don't rise then as they do in winter.

Stretched out along the dry leeward shore, Waikiki rarely has two or three days of rain in a row. If it does rain, it will probably do so in February or March, when the prevailing northeast trade winds subside and are interrupted by southerly or *kona* winds. Looking for a silver lining? If it's raining in Waikiki, the wind shift may mean brilliant sunshine on the windward side of the island, which is normally wetter. Head for beautiful Kailua Beach, for long walks along the strand, swimming, and windsurfing lessons.

Waikiki's hottest months are August and September, although even then, if the temperature hits 90 degrees F (30 degrees C), it makes page one of the newspaper.

Climate   The following are average daily maximum and minimum temperatures for Waikiki.

Jan.	76F	24C	May	80F	27C	Sept.	83F	28C
	68	21		70	21		74	23
Feb.	76F	24C	June	81F	27C	Oct.	82F	28C
	68	19		72	22		72	22
Mar.	77F	25C	July	82F	28C	Nov.	80F	27C
	67	19		73	23		70	21
Apr.	78F	26C	Aug.	83F	28C	Dec.	78F	26C
	68	20		74	23		69	21

Current weather information on over 750 cities around the world—450 of them in the United States—is only a phone call away. Call WeatherTrak at 900/370–8728 from a touch-tone phone—at a cost of 95¢ per minute. The number plays a taped message that tells you to dial a three-digit access code for the destination you're interested in. The code is either the area code (in the United States) or the first three letters of the foreign city. For a list of all access codes, send a stamped, self-addressed envelope to Cities, 9B Terrace Way, Greensboro, NC 27403. For further information, phone 800/247–3282.

Festivals and Seasonal Events

Jan.–Mar.: Narcissus Festival. Welcoming in the Chinese New Year are a queen pageant, coronation ball, cooking demonstrations, and a noisy evening of fireworks in Chinatown.

Jan.–April: Cherry Blossom Festival. A celebration of all things Japanese that includes a run, cultural displays, cooking demonstrations, music, and the inevitable queen pageant with a coronation ball. This festival is well done and popular. Tel. 808/522–4153.

Early Jan.: Queen Emma Museum Open House. To celebrate Queen Emma's birthday, the museum offers free admission. Tel. 808/595–6291.

Mid-Jan.: Hawaiian Open Golf Tournament. The top golf pros tee off for $500,000 in prizes at the exclusive Waialae Country Club.

Mid-Jan.: Hula Bowl. The annual college all-star football classic is played at Aloha Stadium. Special buses often run from Waikiki. Tel. 808/486–9300.

Late Jan.: Robert Burns Night. The clans gather from Canada and mainland United States for a highland fling.

Early Feb.: NFL Pro Bowl. An all-star football game, involving the National and American conferences of the National Football League, is played annually at Aloha Stadium. Tel. 808/486–9300.

Early Feb.: Punahou Carnival. Hawaii's most prestigious school stages an annual fund raiser with rides, arts and crafts, local food, and a great white elephant sale.

Mid-Feb.: Great Aloha Run. An 8-mile course from Aloha Tower to Aloha Stadium benefits the Variety school.

Early Mar.: "World's Greatest Garage and Plant Sale." Crafts and white elephants go on sale to benefit the American Cancer Society. Blaisdell Exhibition Hall, Ward Ave. and King St., tel. 808/522–0333.

Mid-Mar.: Hawaiian Song Festival and Song Composing Contest. The site is Kapiolani Bandstand, Waikiki, tel. 808/521-9815.

Mid-Mar.: Emerald Ball. The Friendly Sons of St. Patrick celebrate with music and dancing.

Mar. 17: St. Patrick's Day Parade. It goes right down Kalakaua Avenue from Fort DeRussy to Kapiolani Park, and is followed by a boisterous no-host party at a Waikiki hotel.

Late Mar.: Opening Day of the Polo Season. Games are held every Sunday through August, 2 PM, at Dillingham Polo Field, Mokuleia, tel. 808/533–2890.

Mar. 26: Prince Kuhio Day. A state holiday honoring Prince Kuhio. Celebration takes place at the Prince Kuhio Federal Building in downtown Honolulu, and at Sea Life Park (tel. 808/259–7933) and Waimea Falls Park (tel. 808/638–8511).

Apr.: Easter Sunrise Service. The Hawaii Council of Churches holds this popular gathering at Punchbowl National Memorial Cemetery of the Pacific. Special buses run to the crater. Tel. 808/531–4888.

Early Apr.: Bud Light Tin Man Biathlon. Athletes test themselves in a 2.7-mile run and 800-meter swim at Ala Moana Park, adjacent to Waikiki.

Mid. Apr.: Buddha Day. Flower pageants are staged at temples throughout the Islands.

Mid. Apr.: Carole Kai Bed Race, Parade, and Concert. Big names in town turn out for this zany event centered in Waikiki. It's all for charity. Tel. 808/735–6092.

May 1: Lei Day. The annual flower-filled celebration is held in Kapiolani Park. Winning leis in the annual lei-making contest are on exhibit. There's music, hula, food—and lots of leis for sale, some of them exquisite floral masterpieces. In the evening, there's a concert of Hawaiian music by the famous local group, the Cazimero Brothers, outdoors at the Waikiki Shell.

Early May: Pacific Handcrafters Guild Spring Fair. Some of Hawaii's best artisans participate. There are demonstrations, food, and entertainment. Ala Moana Park.

Memorial Day: Special military services are held at Punchbowl National Memorial Cemetery of the Pacific. Tel. 808/541–1430.

Late May–early June: Fiftieth State Fair. The Honolulu Jaycees bring together produce exhibits, food booths, entertainment, and amusement rides.

Late May–early June: Festival of the Pacific. A relatively new celebration, this week-long affair of sports, music, songs, and dances has become very popular.

June 11: Kamehameha Day. The Friday before the 11th, the statue of the king who united all the Hawaiian Islands is draped in 25-foot leis. The statue is in downtown Honolulu and makes a great photograph the next morning, when a colorful parade forms at Iolani Palace and proceeds to Ala Moana Park. It's followed by a *ho'olaulea* (street party) in Waikiki.

June–July: Hawaii State Farm Fair. Held on the grounds of Honolulu's McKinley High School, it features farm products, food booths, and amusement rides.

Mid-July: Mid-Summer's Night Gleam. Foster Botanic Garden in downtown Honolulu opens at night for a moonlight walk and entertainment. Tel. 808/537–1708.

Mid-July: Prince Lot Hula Festival. A whole day of ancient and modern hula unfolds beneath the towering trees of Oahu's Moanalua Gardens. Tel. 808/839–5334.

Late July: Annual Ukulele Festival. Hundreds of ukulele players perform at Kapiolani Bandstand in Waikiki.

End of July–Aug. Bon Odori Season. Buddhist temples throughout the Islands invite all to the festivals honoring ancestors. A highlight is the Japanese bon dancing. In mid-July, the Haleiwa Jodo Mission on Oahu's North Shore has a beautiful floating lantern ceremony. Tel. 808/637–4382.

Early Aug.: Makahiki. Hawaiian sports and games, a farm fair, and traditional crafts are featured in this ancient annual celebration. Kapiolani Park, Waikiki.

Early Aug.: Hula Festival. Participants of Honolulu's Summer Fun children's classes plus hula schools (both adults and children) perform at Waikiki's Kapiolani Bandstand on three successive Sundays. Tel. 808/521–9815.

Aug. 19: Admission Day. A state holiday recognizes Hawaii's admission to statehood.

Early Sept.: Waikiki Rough Water Swim. All ages and categories compete in a 2-mile swim to benefit the American Lung Association. Tel. 808/537–5966.

Late Sept.: Aloha Week Festival. Major events include Hawaiian pageantry, canoe races, street parties, entertainment, and a grand parade through Waikiki.

Late Sept.: A Day at Queen Emma Summer Palace. The Daughters of Hawaii stage a day of Hawaiian arts, crafts, and entertainment at the Queen Emma Summer Palace, Honolulu. Tel. 808/595–6291.

Early Oct.: Waimea Falls Park Makahiki. The ancient makahiki was a harvest festival. The tradition is carried out at Waimea Falls Park, Oahu, with a day of games, music, hula competition, and food. Tel. 808/638–8511.

Early Oct.: Pacific Handcrafters Guild Fair. A weekend of craft demonstrations, ethnic foods, and entertainment at Ala Moana Park, Honolulu.

Mid-Oct.: Bankoh Molokai Hoe. The annual Molokai to Oahu canoe race finishes at Fort DeRussy Beach, Waikiki.

Late Aug.: Best Little Chili Cookoff. Honolulu Community Theatre is the beneficiary of this entertaining tasting held at Restaurant Row, near downtown Honolulu. Tel. 808/523–1307.

Mid-Oct.: Orchid Show. It's a beauty at the Blaisdell Center, Honolulu. Tel. 808/527–5400.

End of Nov.: Mission Houses Museum Annual Christmas Fair. Artists and craftspeople present their wares in an open market at the historic houses of Hawaii's first Yankee missionaries in downtown Honolulu. Tel. 808/531–0481.

Nov.–early Dec.: Hawaii International Film Festival. A visual feast of award-winning cinematography from the United States, Asia, and the Pacific illustrates the theme "When Strangers Meet." Several theaters in Waikiki participate. Tel. 808/944–7200.

Dec.: Triple Crown of Surfing. Times, dates, and beaches are based on wave conditions as the top pro surfers gather for the winter waves on Oahu's North Shore. All month.

Early Dec.: Pacific Handcrafters Guild Christmas Fair. Here's a chance to buy some inexpensive art for gifts. Thomas Square, Honolulu.

Early Dec.: Honolulu Marathon. Watch or join this 26.2-mile event which annually draws 8,000–10,000 runners.

Early Dec.: Bodhi Day. The Buddhist community celebrates the Day of Enlightenment.

Dec. 25: Christmas. The hotels outdo each other in extravagant exhibits. When local children are small, part of their holiday treat is going from lobby to lobby to see the fantastic displays—towering poinsettia trees (Kahala Hilton, Ilikai), Santa arriving by outrigger (Kahala Hilton), and a gingerbread town (Hyatt Regency), to name a few of the most memorable. There are concerts by children's choirs and special treats for guest children. Christmas won't be white, but it will be very merry.

Christmas Day: Eagle Aloha Bowl. The popular game is a collegiate event at Aloha Stadium, Oahu. Tel. 808/488–9509.

What to Pack

You can pack lightly because Hawaii is casual. Bare feet, bathing suits, and comfortable, informal clothing are the norm.

The Man's Suitcase In the Hawaiian Islands, there's a saying that when a man wears a suit during the day, he's either going for a loan or he's a lawyer trying a case. Only a few upscale Waikiki restaurants require a jacket for dinner, and none requires a tie. Hawaii regulars wear their jackets on the plane—just in case—and many don't put them on again until the return flight. The aloha shirt is accepted dress in Hawaii for business and most social occasions. A visitor can easily buy one after arriving in Waikiki (*see* Chapter 5).

Shorts are acceptable daytime attire, along with a T-shirt or polo shirt. If you want to be marked as a tourist, wear your shorts with dark shoes and white socks. Local-style casual footwear consists of tennis or running shoes, sandals, or rubber slippers. You'll also see a lot of bare feet, but state law requires that footwear be worn in all food establishments.

Pack your toiletries, underwear, and a pair or two of easy-care slacks to wear with those aloha shirts, and you're all set.

Female Fashion   During the winter months, be sure to bring a sweater or wrap for the evening because the trade winds cool things off as soon as the sun goes down. If you have an elaborate coiffure, a scarf will help keep it from getting windblown.

Sundresses, shorts, and tops are fine for daytime. During the summer months, synthetic slacks and shirts, although easy to care for, can get uncomfortably warm. If you have a long slip, bring it for the muumuu you say you won't buy, but probably will. As for shoes, sandals and tennis or running shoes are fine for daytime, and sandals are perfect for the evening. If you wear boots, you'll wish you hadn't.

If you don't own a pareu, buy one in Hawaii. It's simply a length (about 1½ yards long) of light cotton in a tropical motif that can be worn as a beachwrap, a skirt, or a dozen other wrap-up fashions. A pareu is useful wherever you go, regardless of climate. It makes a good bathrobe, so you don't have to pack one. You can even tie it up as a handbag or sit on it at the beach.

For Everyone   Don't forget your bathing suit. Sooner or later, the crystal clear water tempts even the most sedentary landlubber. Of course, bathing suits are easy to find in Hawaii. Shops are crammed with the latest styles. If you wear a bathing cap, bring one; you can waste hours searching for one.

Probably the most important thing to tuck in your suitcase is sunscreen. This is the tropics, and the ultraviolet rays are much more powerful than those to which you are accustomed. Doctors advise putting on sunscreen when you get up in the morning. Women can wear it as a moisturizer under makeup. The upper chest area of a woman is hypopigmented and should be protected. Don't forget to reapply sunscreen periodically during the day, since perspiration can wash it away. Consider using sunscreens with a sun protection factor (SPF) of 15 or higher. There are many tanning oils on the market in Hawaii, including coconut and kukui oils, but doctors warn that they merely sauté your skin. Too many Hawaiian vacations have been spoiled by sunburn.

Visitors who wear glasses are wise to pack an extra pair. Eyeglasses are easy to lose, and you can waste your precious Hawaiian holiday replacing them. If the worst happens, several while-you-wait lens shops can ease your eye strain.

If you don't bring your camera and plenty of film, you'll wish you did. Much of Hawaii is so beautiful that all you have to do is point and shoot to get great photographs. Overnight processing is available at many locations in Waikiki.

It's a good idea to tuck in a few jumbo zip-lock plastic bags when you travel—they're ideal for wet swimsuits or food souvenirs that might leak. All hotels in Hawaii provide beach towels. Some hotels provide hair dryers and some don't. Unless you know for sure, bring your own. If you forget something, you can probably find it at your hotel sundry store or at one of the ever-present ABC drugstores in and around Waikiki.

Cash Machines

Virtually all U.S. banks belong to a network of ATMs (Automatic Teller Machines), which gobble up bank cards and spit out cash 24 hours a day in cities throughout the country. There are some eight major networks in the United States, the largest of which are Cirrus, owned by MasterCard, and Plus, affiliated with Visa. Some banks belong to more than one network. These cards are not automatically issued; you have to ask for them. If your bank doesn't belong to at least one network, you should consider moving your account, for ATMs are becoming as essential as check cashing. Cards issued by Visa and MasterCard may also be used in the ATMs, but the fees are usually higher than the fees on bank cards, and there is a daily interest charge on the "loan," even if monthly bills are paid on time. Each network has a toll-free number you can call to locate machines in a given city. The Cirrus number is 800/4–CIRRUS; the Plus number is 800/THE–PLUS. Check with your bank for fees and for the amount of cash you can withdraw on any given day.

Waikiki has cash machines at **Bank of Hawaii** (2220 Kalakaua Ave.), **Central Pacific Bank** (Hyatt Regency Hotel, 2424 Kalakaua Ave.), **City Bank** (2301 Kuhio St.), **First Hawaiian Bank** (2181 Kalakaua Ave.), **First Nationwide Bank** (334 Seaside Ave.), **Hawaii National Bank** (321 Seaside Ave.), and **Liberty Bank** (Royal Hawaiian Shopping Center). Before you leave home, ask your local bank for a list of banks in Hawaii that will honor your bank cash card.

Insurance

Travelers may seek insurance coverage in three areas: health and accident, loss of luggage, and trip cancellation. Your first step is to review your existing health and homeowner policies; some health insurance plans cover health expenses incurred while traveling, some major medical plans cover emergency transportation, and some homeowner policies cover the theft of luggage.

Health and Accident Several companies offer coverage designed to supplement existing health insurance for travelers:

Carefree Travel Insurance (Box 310, 120 Mineola Blvd., Mineola, NY 11501, tel. 516/294–0220 or 800/323–3149) provides coverage for emergency medical evacuation and accidental death and dismemberment. It also offers 24-hour medical phone advice.

International SOS Assistance (Box 11568, Philadelphia, PA 19116, tel. 215/244–1500 or 800/523–8930), a medical assistance company, provides emergency evacuation services, worldwide medical referrals, and optional medical insurance.

Travel Guard International, underwritten by Transamerica Occidental Life Companies (1145 Clark St., Stevens Point, WI 54481, tel. 715/345–0505 or 800/782–5151) offers reimbursement for emergency evacuation services and medical expenses with no deductibles or daily limits.

Wallach and Company, Inc. (243 Church St., NW, Suite 100D, Vienna, VA 22180, tel. 703/281–9500 or 800/237–6615), offers comprehensive medical coverage, including emergency evacuation services worldwide.

For British Travelers   We recommend that to cover health and motoring mishaps, you insure yourself with **Europ Assistance** (252 High St., Croydon, Surrey CRO INF, tel. 081/680–1234).

Lost Luggage   The loss of luggage is usually covered as part of a comprehensive travel insurance package that includes personal accident, trip cancellation, and sometimes default and bankruptcy insurance. Several companies offer comprehensive policies:

Access America Inc., a subsidiary of Blue Cross-Blue Shield (Box 11188, Richmond, VA 23230, tel. 800/334–7525 or 800/284–8300).
Near Services, (450 Prairie Ave., Suite 101, Calumet City, IL 60409, tel. 708/868–6700 or 800/654–6700).
Travel Guard International (*see* Health and Accident Insurance above).

For British Travelers   It is also wise to take out insurance to cover the loss of luggage (although check that such loss isn't already covered in any existing homeowner's policies you may have). Trip-cancellation insurance is another wise buy. **The Association of British Insurers** (Aldermary House, 10–15 Queen St., London EC4N 1TT, tel. 071/248–4477) will give comprehensive advice on all aspects of vacation insurance.

Trip Cancellation   Flight insurance is often included in the price of a ticket when paid for with American Express, Visa, and other major credit and charge cards. It is usually included in combination travel insurance packages available from most tour operators, travel agents, and insurance agents.

Traveling with Film

If your camera is new, shoot and develop a few rolls of film before leaving home. Pack some lens tissue and an extra battery for your built-in light meter. Invest about $10 in a skylight filter and screw it onto the front of your lens. It will protect the lens and reduce haze.

Film doesn't survive hot weather. If you're driving in summer, don't store film in the glove compartment or on the shelf under the rear window. Put it behind the front seat on the floor, on the side opposite the exhaust pipe.

On a plane trip, never pack unprocessed film in check-in luggage; if your bags get X-rayed, say goodbye to your pictures. Always carry undeveloped film with you through airport security and ask to have it inspected by hand. (It helps to isolate your film in a plastic bag, ready for quick inspection.) Inspectors at American airports are required by law to honor requests for hand inspection.

The newer airport scanning machines—used in all U.S. airports—are safe for anything from five to 500 scans, depending on the speed of your film. The effects are cumulative; you can put the same roll of film through several scans without worry. After five scans, though, you're asking for trouble.

If your film gets fogged and you want an explanation, send it to the National Association of Photographic Manufacturers (550

Mamaroneck Ave., Harrison, NY 10528), which will try to determine what went wrong. The service is free.

Traveling with Children

Publications *Family Travel Times*, an 8- to 12-page newsletter, is published 10 times a year by TWYCH (Travel with Your Children, 80 Eighth Ave., New York, NY 10011, tel. 212/206–0688). Subscription includes access to back issues and twice-weekly opportunities to call in for specific advice. *Great Vacations with Your Kids: The Complete Guide to Family Vacations in the U.S.* by Dorothy Ann Jordon and Marjorie Adoff Cohen (E. P. Dutton, New York) details everything from city vacations to adventure vacations to child-care resources.

Condo Rentals See *The Condo Lux Vacationer's Guide to Condominium Rentals in the Southwest and Hawaii* by Jill Little (Vintage Books/Random House, New York).

Home Exchange See *Home Exchanging: A Complete Sourcebook for Travelers at Home or Abroad* by James Dearing (Globe Pequot Press, Box Q, Chester, CT 06412, tel. 800/243–0495; in CT, tel. 800/962–0973).

Getting There On domestic flights, children under 2 who are not occupying a seat travel free. Various discounts apply to children ages 2–12. Regulations about infant travel on airplanes are in the process of changing. Until they do, however, if you want to be sure your infant is secured in his/her own safety seat, you must buy a separate ticket and bring your own infant car seat. (Check with the airline in advance; certain seats aren't allowed. Or write for the booklet *Child/Infant Safety Seats Acceptable for Use in Aircraft*, from the Federal Aviation Administration, APA-200, 800 Independence Ave. SW, Washington, DC 20591, tel. 202/267–3479.) Some airlines allow babies to travel in their own safety seats at no charge if there's a spare seat on the plane available, otherwise safety seats will be stored and the child will have to be held by a parent. If you opt to hold your baby on your lap, do so with the infant outside the seat belt so he or she won't be crushed in case of a sudden stop.

Also inquire about special children's meals or snacks. See the February 1990 and 1992 issues of *Family Travel Times* for "TWYCH's Airline Guide," which contains a rundown of the children's services offered by 46 airlines.

In the Waikiki Area Some hotels in and around Waikiki offer special programs for children, which are supervised by adults. These programs may include such activities as arts and crafts, sports, and treasure hunts. Among the hotels offering programs for children are the Hilton Hawaiian Village, the Kahala Hilton, and the Sheraton Waikiki (*see* Chapter 8 for addresses and numbers). About 2,500 children annually participate in Sheraton's "Keiki Aloha Program," headquartered at the Sheraton Waikiki and offered free to guests of all Sheraton hotels in Waikiki. The imaginative program includes evening activities so parents may dine and dance on their own. You may wish to find out beforehand if the hotel you are planning to stay at has special programs for children.

Car Rental Hawaii state law requires that infants be restrained in car seats. Check to be sure your rental company has a seat available for you.

Hints for Disabled Travelers

The Information Center for Individuals with Disabilities (Fort Point Pl., 1st floor, 27-43 Wormwood St., Boston, MA 02110, tel. 617/727–5540; TDD 617/727–5236) offers useful problem-solving assistance, including lists of travel agents who specialize in tours for the disabled.

Moss Rehabilitation Hospital Travel Information Service (1200 W. Tabor Rd., Philadelphia, PA 19141–3009, tel. 215/456–9600; TDD 215/456–9602) provides information on tourist sights, transportation, and accommodations in destinations around the world. The fee is $5 for each destination. Allow one month for delivery.

Mobility International USA (Box 3551, Eugene, OR 97403, tel. 503/343–1284) has information on accommodations, organized study, and so forth around the world.

The Society for the Advancement of Travel for the Handicapped (26 Court St., Brooklyn, NY 11242, tel. 718/858–5483) offers access information. The annual membership is $45 or $25 for senior travelers and students. Send $1 and a stamped, self-addressed envelope.

The Itinerary (Box 1084, Bayonne, NJ 07002, tel. 201/858–3400) is a bimonthly travel magazine for the disabled.

Greyhound/Trailways (tel. 800/752–4841) will carry a disabled person and a companion for the price of a single fare. Amtrak (tel. 800/USA–RAIL) requests 48-hour notice to provide red-cap service, special seats, and a 25% discount (disabled children and elderly passengers are entitled to additional reductions). It is wise to check the price of excursion tickets first, as these are often cheaper than disabled reductions on regular tickets. For a free copy of *Access Amtrak*, a guide to special services for elderly and disabled travelers, write to Amtrak (National Railroad Corp., 400 N. Capital St., Washington, DC 20001).

In the Waikiki Area Many of Hawaii's major attractions, shopping centers, and restaurants have wheelchair ramps, and the better hotels offer entry and exit ramps, grab bars, low telephones, and parking stalls. The Commission on Persons with Disabilities (5 Waterfront Plaza, Suite 210, 500 Ala Moana Blvd., Honolulu 96813, tel. 808/548–7606) offers a free *Traveler's Guide*, with information to help the disabled plan a visit to Hawaii. Included are listings of facilities and their accessibility features and a mobility map of Waikiki.

You can pick up a handicapped-parking pass at the Department of Transportation Services (650 S. King St., Honolulu 96813, tel. 808/523–4021). If you already have a windshield card from your own state, that's all you need. Curb-to-curb service is offered through Aloha-State Tour & Transportation Co. Ltd., operating as Handi-Vans (tel. 808/924–2634 or 848–4444) if it is arranged on a 24-hour notice. You must meet the Handi-vans administrator once in person, however, to prove your disability. All rides cost $1 one-way. Handi-Cabs of the Pacific (tel. 808/524–3866) is a private taxi company with van ramps. It operates on Oahu for an $8 curbside pickup charge plus $1.95 per mile, and offers free wheelchairs to transfer passengers. Avis (tel. 800/331–1212) rents hand controls for cars. Wheelchairs, walkers, oxygen, lifts, and overbed tables can be rented from AA Medical Equipment (711 S. Queen St., Honolulu 96813, tel. 808/537–5933) and Abbey Medical (500 Ala Kawa St., Honolulu,

96817, tel. 808/845–5000). You must contact these companies in advance.

Hints for Older Travelers

The American Association of Retired Persons (AARP, 1909 K St. NW, Washington, DC 20049, tel. 202/662–4850) has two programs for independent travelers: (1) The Purchase Privilege Program, which offers discounts on hotels, airfare, car rentals, and sightseeing, and (2) the AARP Motoring Plan, provided by Amoco, which offers emergency aid and trip-routing information for an annual fee of $29.95 per couple. AARP members must be age 50 or older. Annual dues are $5 per person or per couple.

When using an AARP or other identification card, ask for a reduced hotel rate at the time you make your reservation, not when you check out. At participating restaurants, show your card to the maître d' before you're seated, since discounts may be limited to certain set menus, days, or hours. When renting a car, remember that economy cars, priced at promotional rates, may cost less than cars that are available with your ID card.

Elderhostel (75 Federal St., 3rd floor, Boston, MA 02110–1914, tel. 617/426–7788) is an innovative 13-year-old program for people aged 60 and older. Participants live in dormitories on some 1,200 campuses around the world. Mornings are devoted to lectures and seminars; afternoons, to sightseeing and field trips. The all-inclusive fee for 2–3 week trips, including room, board, tuition, and round-trip transportation, is $1,700–$3,200.

Golden Age Passport is a free lifetime pass to all parks, monuments, and recreation areas run by the federal government. People over age 61 may pick it up in person at any national park that charges admission. A driver's license or other proof of age is required.

Mature Outlook (6001 N. Clark St., Chicago, IL 60660, tel. 800/336–6330), a subsidiary of Sears Roebuck & Co., is a travel club for people over age 50, with hotel and motel discounts and a bimonthly newsletter. Annual membership is $9.95 per couple. Instant membership is available at participating Holiday Inns.

National Council of Senior Citizens (925 15th St. NW, Washington, DC 20005, tel. 202/347–8800) is a nonprofit advocacy group with some 5,000 local clubs across the country. Annual membership is $12 per person or per couple. Members receive a monthly newspaper with travel information and an ID card for reduced-rate hotels and car rentals.

Travel Industry and Disabled Exchange (TIDE, 5435 Donna Ave., Tarzana, CA 91356, tel. 818/343–6339) is an industry-based organization with a $15 per person annual membership fee. Members receive a quarterly newsletter and information on travel agencies and tours.

Hawaiian Language

The Hawaiian language is unlike anything normally heard by the average traveler. But given the chance, say at a traditional church service or a local ceremony, visitors will find the soft, rolling language of the Islands both interesting and refreshing to the ear.

Although an understanding of Hawaiian is by no means required, *malihinis*, or newcomers, will find plenty of opportunities to pick up a few of the local words and phrases. In fact, traditional names and expressions are still in such wide usage today that visitors will be hard pressed not to read or hear them each day of their visit. Such exposure adds nothing but enrichment to any stay. With a basic understanding and some uninhibited practice, anyone can have enough command of the local tongue to ask for directions by street names and to order off the neighborhood restaurant menus.

Simplifying the learning process is the fact that the Hawaiian language contains only seven consonants—H, K, L, M, N, P, and W—and the five vowels. All syllables and all words end in a vowel. Each vowel, with the exception of diphthongized double vowels such as *au* (pronounced ow) or *ai* (pronounced eye), is pronounced separately. *Aa*, the word for rough lava, for example, is pronounced ah-ah.

Although some Hawaiian words have only vowels, most also contain some combination consonants as well. Consonants are never doubled, and they always begin syllables, as in Ka-me-ha-me-ha.

The accent in most Hawaiian words falls on the penultimate syllable. Since most Hawaiian words are two syllables, the accent falls on the first syllable as in KO-na, PA-li, and KA-na. The exception occurs when the vowels in the second syllable become diphthongized, as in ha-PAI and ma-KAI, which are fundamentally ha-PA-i and ma-KA-i.

Pronunciation is simple. Use the following table as a guide to pronounce

A "uh" as in above
E "ay" as in weigh
I "ee" as in marine
O "oh" as in no
U "oo" as in true

Consonants mirror their English equivalents, with the exception of W. When the letter begins the last syllable of a word, it is sometimes pronounced as a V. Awa, the Polynesian drink, is pronounced "ava"; Ewa plantation is pronounced "Eva."

What follows is a glossary of some of the most commonly used Hawaiian words. Don't be afraid to give them a try. Hawaii residents appreciate visitors who at least try to pick up the local language—no matter how fractured the pronunciation.

aa—rough, crumbling lava, contrasting with *pahoehoe*, which is smooth.
ae—yes.
akamai—smart, clever, possessing savoir-faire.
ala—a road, path, or trail.
alii—a Hawaiian chief, a member of the chiefly class; also plural.
aloha—love, affection, kindness. Also a salutation meaning both greetings and farewell.
aole—no.
auwai—a ditch.
auwe—alas, woe is me!
ehu—a red-haired Hawaiian.
ewa—in the direction of Ewa plantation, west of Honolulu.

hala—the pandanus tree, whose leaves *(lauhala)* are used to make baskets and plaited mats.

hale—a house.

hana—to work.

haole—originally a stranger or foreigner. Since the first foreigners were Caucasian, *haole* now means a Caucasian person.

hapa—a part, sometimes a half.

hapa haole—part *haole*, a person of mixed racial background, part of which is Caucasian.

hauoli—to rejoice. *Hauoli Makahiki Hou* means Happy New Year.

heiau—an ancient Hawaiian place of worship.

holo—to run.

holoholo—to go for a walk, ride, or sail.

holoku—a long Hawaiian dress, somewhat fitted, with a scoop neck and a train. Influenced by European fashion, it was worn at court.

holomuu—a recent cross between a *holoku* and a *muumuu*, less fitted than the former but less voluminous than the latter, and having no train.

honi—to kiss, a kiss. A phrase that some tourists may find useful, quoted from a popular *hula*, is *Honi Kaua wikiwiki:* Kiss me quick!

hoomalimali—flattery, a deceptive "line," bunk, baloney, hooey.

huhu—angry.

hui—a group, club, or assembly. There are church *huis* and social *huis*.

hukilau—a seine, a communal fishing party in which everyone helps to drive the fish into a huge net, pull it in, and divide the catch.

hula—the dance of Hawaii.

ipo—sweetheart.

ka—the definite article.

kahuna—a priest, doctor, or other trained person of old Hawaii, endowed with special professional skills that often included the gift of prophecy or other supernatural powers.

kai—the sea, salt water.

kalo—the taro plant from whose root *poi* is made.

kamaaina—literally, a child of the soil, it refers to people who were born in the Islands or have lived there for a long time.

kanaka—originally a man or humanity in general, it is now used to denote a male Hawaiian or part-Hawaiian.

kane—a man, a husband. If you see this word on a door, it's the men's room.

kapa—also called *tapa*, a cloth made of beaten bark and usually dyed and stamped with a primitive geometric design.

kapakahi—crooked, cockeyed, uneven. You've got your hat on *kapakahi*.

kapu—keep out, prohibited. This is the Hawaiian version of the more widely known Tongan word *tabu* (taboo).

keiki—a child; *keikikane* is a boy child, *keikiwahine* a girl.

kokua—help.

kona—the south, also the south or leeward side of the islands from which the *kona* wind and *kona* rain come.

kuleana—a homestead or small plot of ground on which a family has been installed for some generations without necessarily owning it. By extension, *kuleana* is used to denote any area or department in which one has a special interest or prerogative. You'll hear it used this way: If you want to hire a surfboard, see

Moki; that's his *kuleana.* And conversely, I can't help you with that; that's not my *kuleana.*
lamalama—to fish with a torch.
lanai—a porch, a covered pavilion, an outdoor living room. Almost every house in Hawaii has one.
lani—heaven, the sky.
lauhala—the leaf of the *hala* or pandanus tree, widely used in Hawaiian handcrafts.
lei—a garland of flowers.
luna—a plantation overseer or foreman.
mahalo—thank you.
makai—toward the sea.
malihini—a newcomer to the Islands.
mana—the spiritual power that the Hawaiians believed to inhabit all things and creatures.
manawahi—free, gratis.
mauka—toward the mountains.
mauna—mountain.
mele—a Hawaiian song or chant, often of epic proportions.
menehune—a Hawaiian pixie. The *menehunes* were a legendary race of little people who accomplished prodigious work, like building fishponds and temples in the course of a single night.
moana—the ocean.
muumuu—the voluminous dress in which the missionaries enveloped Hawaiian women. Now made up in bright printed cottons and silks, it is an indispensable garment in a Hawaiian woman's wardrobe.
nani—beautiful.
nui—big.
pake—a Chinese. Give this *pake* boy some rice.
palapala—book, printing.
pali—a cliff, precipice.
panini—cactus.
paniolo—a Hawaiian cowboy.
pau—finished, done.
pilikia—trouble. The Hawaiian word is much more widely used here than its English equivalent.
puka—a hole.
pupule—crazy, like the celebrated Princess Pupule. This word has replaced its English equivalent in local usage.
wahine—a female, a woman, a wife, and a sign on the ladies' room door.
wai—fresh water, as opposed to salt water, which is *kai.*
wikiwiki—to hurry, hurry up.

Pidgin English is the unofficial language of Hawaii. It is heard everywhere: on ranches, in warehouses, on beaches, and in the hallowed halls (though not in the classrooms) of the University of Hawaii. It's still English and not much tougher to follow than Brooklynese; it just takes a little getting used to.

Further Reading

For a good historical and adventure novel set on the Hawaiian Islands, start with *Hawaii*, by James A. Michener. Other works of fiction set in the Hawaiian Islands include Margaret M. Dukore's *Bloom*, a romance set in Honolulu; *Death March* by Ralph Glendinning, a suspense novel; *Waimea Summer* by John Dominis Holt, an autobiographical novel about a boy's experiences in Hawaii; James Jones's novel *From Here to Eternity*, about army life in pre-Pearl Harbor days; Jack London's *Stories of Hawaii;* Kathleen Mellen's *In a Hawaiian Valley*, stories of Hawaiian home life (currently out of print, but worth looking for in a library); and N. Richard Nash's *East Wind, Rain*, a novel of love and espionage at Pearl Harbor, 1941.

Garrett Hongo often writes about Hawaii in his two poetry collections, *Yellow Light* and *The River of Heaven*. Two anthologies of Hawaii-related literature include *A Hawaiian Reader* and *The Spell of Hawaii*, both edited by A. Grove Day and Carl Stroven.

Hawaii's history may be explored in Gwenfread Allen's *Hawaii's War Years, 1941–1945;* Paul Bailey's *Those Kings and Queens of Old Hawaii; Shoal of Time*, Gavan Davis's history of the Hawaiian Islands; and Edward Joesting's *Hawaii: An Uncommon History*. Two other nonfiction books worth investigating are Robert Louis Stevenson's *Travels in Hawaii* and Mark Twain's *Letters from Hawaii*.

Now in its 14th year of publication, *ALOHA, The Magazine of Hawaii and the Pacific* (49 S. Hotel St., Suite 309, Honolulu, HI 96813, 808/523–9871), is a valuable source of information about the Fiftieth State and other Pacific destinations; it covers a wide range of topics including history, the arts, business, people, sports, food, interiors, music and dance, flora and fauna, Pacific-related books, and real estate. *ALOHA* is a bimonthly publication; subscription rates are $14.95 a year (six issues). *Pacific Art & Travel* (891 Eha St., Suite 201, Wailuku, Maui, HI 96793) features artist profiles and travel articles relevant to Hawaii and the Pacific. An up-to-date dining guide, a date book of happenings, and a shopping-treasures section make this beautifully rendered magazine useful as well. *Pacific Art & Travel* is published quarterly; subscription rates are $12 per year.

Arriving and Departing

By Plane

From the Mainland United States Honolulu International Airport is one of the busiest in the nation. It has been completely renovated and is only 20 minutes from Waikiki. Flying time from the West Coast is 4½–5 hours.

American carriers serving Hawaii include **United, Northwest, American, Continental, Delta, TWA, Hawaiian, Pan Am, Air America, Trans Continental Airlines,** and **America West.** Most flights to Hawaii originate in Los Angeles or San Francisco, which, of course, means they are nonstop. There are also nonstop flights from Dallas/Fort Worth, Chicago, Seattle, San Diego, and St. Louis. There are direct flights (which means there are one or more stops along the route, but you don't have to change planes) from Anchorage, New York, and other cities in the East, Southwest, and Midwest. Connecting flights are available from almost every American city.

By law, foreign carriers serving Hawaii may not carry passengers from other American cities. Bringing passengers from foreign destinations are **Qantas, Canadian Pacific Air, Air Canada, Japan Air Lines, Philippine Air Lines, Air New Zealand,**

China Air Lines, Korean Air Lines, Singapore Airlines, Air Tungaru, Air Niugini, All Nippon Airways, UTA French Airlines, Air Micronesia, Canadian Air Lines International, Garuda Indonesia, and Malaysian Airlines.

From the United Kingdom American, Continental, Delta, and TWA are among the airlines that fly to Honolulu. An APEX ticket costs about £559 for a midweek flight, plus taxes. Ring around for the best offers.

Trailfinders (42–48 Earl's Court Rd., Kensington, London W8 6EJ, tel. 071/938–3366) can arrange flights to Honolulu from £535.

Discount Flights Charter flights are the least expensive and the least reliable—with chronically late departures and occasional cancellations. They also tend to depart less frequently (usually once a week) than do regularly scheduled flights. If the savings are worth the potential annoyance, charter flights serving Honolulu International Airport include Air America (808/834–7172 or 800/323–8052) and Trans Air (808/833–5557). Consult your local travel agent for further information.

Smoking Smoking is banned on all routes within the 48 contiguous states; within the states of Hawaii and Alaska; to and from the U.S. Virgin Islands and Puerto Rico; and on flights of less than six hours to and from Hawaii and Alaska. The rule applies to both domestic and foreign carriers.

On a flight where smoking is permitted, you can request a nonsmoking seat during check-in or when you book your ticket. If the airline tells you there are no seats available in the nonsmoking section, insist on one: Department of Transportation regulations require carriers to find seats for all nonsmokers, provided they meet check-in time restrictions. These regulations apply to all international flights on domestic carriers; however, the Department of Transportation does not have jurisdiction over foreign carriers traveling out of, or into, the United States.

Carry-on Luggage New rules have been in effect since January 1, 1988, on U.S. airlines regarding carry-on luggage. The model for these new rules was agreed to by the airlines in December 1987 and then circulated by the Air Transport Association with the understanding that each airline would present its own version.

Under the model, passengers are limited to two carry-on bags. For a bag you wish to store under the seat, the maximum dimensions are 9″ × 14″ × 22″, a total of 45″. For bags that can be hung in a closet or on a luggage rack, the maximum dimensions are 4″ × 23″ × 45″, a total of 72″. For bags you wish to store in an overhead bin, the maximum dimensions are 10″ × 14″ × 36″, a total of 60″. Your two carryons must each fit one of these sets of dimensions, and any item that exceeds the specified dimensions will generally be rejected as a carryon and handled as checked baggage. Keep in mind that an airline can adapt these rules to circumstances, so on an especially crowded flight, don't be surprised if you are allowed only one carry-on bag.

In addition to the two carryons, the rules list eight items that may also be brought aboard: a handbag (pocketbook or purse), an overcoat or wrap, an umbrella, a camera, a reasonable amount of reading material, an infant bag, crutches, a cane, braces, or other prosthetic devices. An infant/child safety seat can also be brought aboard if parents have purchased a ticket for the child or if there is space in the cabin.

Note that these regulations are for U.S. airlines only. Foreign airlines generally allow one piece of carry-on luggage in tourist class in addition to handbags and bags filled with duty-free goods. Passengers in first and business class are also allowed to carry on one garment bag. It is best to check with the airline ahead of time to find out its exact rules regarding carry-on luggage.

Checked Luggage U.S. airlines allow passengers to check in two suitcases whose total dimensions (length plus width plus height) do not exceed 60″, and whose weight does not exceed 70 pounds.

Rules governing foreign airlines vary from airline to airline, so check with your travel agent or the airline itself before you go. All the airlines allow passengers to check in two bags. In general, expect the weight restriction on the two bags to be not more than 70 lbs. each, and the size restriction on each bag to be not more than 62″ total dimensions.

Luggage Insurance Airlines are responsible for lost or damaged property only up to $1,250 per passenger on domestic flights, $9.07 per pound (or $20 per kilo) for checked baggage on international flights, and up to $400 per passenger for unchecked baggage on international flights. If you're carrying valuables, either take them with you on the airplane or purchase extra insurance for lost luggage. Some airlines will issue additional luggage insurance when you check in, but many do not. One that does is **American Airlines.** Its additional insurance is only for domestic flights or flights to Canada. The rate is $1 for every $100 valuation, with a maximum of $400 valuation per passenger; hand luggage is not included.

Insurance for lost, damaged, or stolen luggage is available through travel agents or directly through various insurance companies. Two that issue luggage insurance are **Tele-Trip** (tel. 800/228–9792), a subsidiary of Mutual of Omaha, and **The Travelers Insurance Co.** Tele-Trip operates sales booths at airports and issues insurance through travel agents. Tele-Trip will insure checked luggage for up to 180 days and for $500–$3,000 valuation. For 1–3 days, the rate for a $500 valuation is $8.25; for 180 days, $100. The Travelers Insurance Co. will insure checked or hand luggage for $500–$2,000 valuation per person, also for a maximum of 180 days. The rate for 1–5 days for $500 valuation is $10; for 180 days, $85. For more information, write: The Travelers Insurance Co., Ticket and Travel Dept., 1 Tower Sq., Hartford, CT 06183. Both companies offer the same rates on domestic and international flights. Check the travel pages of your Sunday newspaper for the names of other companies that insure luggage. Before you go, itemize the contents of each bag in case you need to file an insurance claim. Be certain to put your home address on each piece of luggage, including carry-on bags. If your luggage is stolen and later recovered, the airline must deliver the luggage to your home free of charge.

Between the Airport and Waikiki There are taxis right at the airport exit. At $1.75 start-up plus 25¢ for each ⅐ mile, the fare will run approximately $20 plus a tip. Drivers are also allowed to charge 30¢ per suitcase. **Terminal Transportation** runs an airport shuttle service to Waikiki (tel. 808/836–0317. Cost: $5). The municipal bus is only 60¢, but you are allowed only one bag which must fit on your lap. Some hotels have their own pickup service. Check when you book your reservations.

If you have extra time at the airport, you will be able to visit the new **Pacific Aerospace Museum** (tel. 808/531–7747) on the upper level of the central concourse of the main terminal. At press time it was still not opened, and a report was unavailable.

Lei Greeting Many visitors are disappointed to find that everyone arriving in Hawaii is not automatically given a lei. With the visitor count at almost 6 million, doing so would bankrupt the state. If you have booked through a tour company and are being met at the airport, you will probably be given a lei by the person who meets you. If you have friends meeting you, most definitely they will have a lei for you. If you are traveling independently, you can arrange for a lei greeting from **Greeters of Hawaii** (Box 29638, Honolulu 96820, tel. 808/836–0161); it requires 48 hours notice. Cost: $14.95 to $39.95 per person, add $10 for late notification. The standard $14.95 lei usually contains orchids or an orchid-carnation mixture. Being draped in flowers is definitely one of the pleasures of arriving in the Islands. Surprise your traveling companion.

By Ship

Boat Day used to be the biggest day of the week. Jet travel has almost obscured that custom, and it's too bad, because arriving in Hawaii by ship is a great experience. If you have the time, it is one sure way to unwind. Many cruises are planned a year or more in advance and fill up fast. Because of customs regulations, if you sail on a foreign ship from any U.S. port, you must return with that ship to that port. If you arrive in Hawaii from a foreign port, you may disembark in Honolulu. Most cruiseship companies today offer a fare that includes round-trip air travel to the point of embarkation.

Cunard/N.A.C. Line, Royal Cruises, P & O/Princess Cruises and **Royal Viking** have cruise ships passing through Honolulu once or twice a year.

Car Rentals

The cost of shipping a car by freighter is at least $500. We advise leaving your car at home and renting one.

There's absolutely no need to rent a car if you don't plan to leave Waikiki. In fact, it will be a nuisance with all the one-way streets and the difficulty in parking. If you plan to do some sightseeing outside Waikiki, a number of highly competitive rental-car companies offer special deals and discount coupons. When you're booking your hotel or plane reservations, ask if there is a car tie-in. The Hawaii State Consumer Protection Office also suggests that on fly/drive deals, you ask (1) whether the company will honor a reservation rate if only larger cars are available when you arrive, and (2) whether only certain credit cards will be accepted. **Hertz, Avis, National,** and **Dollar** systems have tie-ins with Hawaiian Air; **Budget** ties in with Aloha Airlines.

During peak seasons—summer, Christmas vacation, and February—car reservations are necessary.

Rental agencies abound in and around the Honolulu Airport and in Waikiki. Often it is cheaper to rent in Waikiki than at the airport. Expect to pay around $35–$45 daily at the airport and $30–$40 in Waikiki, with lower rates at local budget companies. On Oahu, unlimited mileage is often the rule. At press time, Dollar had the best daily rate and Budget the best weekly rate.

Avis (tel. 800/331–1212), **Hertz** (tel. 800/654–3131), **Budget** (tel. 800/527–0700), **Thrifty** (tel. 800/367–2277), **National** (tel. 800/328–4567), **Sears** (tel. 800/527–0770), and **Dollar** (tel. 800/421–6868) have airport and downtown offices. Local budget and used-rental-car companies include **Tropical** (tel. 808/836–1041), which serves other islands, too; **Roberts Hawaii** (tel. 808/947–3939), which will rent to married 18-year-olds; **Five-O** (tel. 808/695–5266), with special deals for members of the armed forces; **VIP** (tel. 808/946–1671); **Island World** (tel. 808/839–2222), another multi-island company.

Find out a few essentials *before* you arrive at the rental counter. (Otherwise a sales agent could talk you into additional costs you don't need.) The major added cost in renting cars is usually the so-called collision damage waiver (CDW). Find out from the rental agency you're planning to use what the waiver will cover. Your own employee or personal insurance may already cover the damage to a rental car. If so, bring along a photocopy of the benefits section of your insurance policy.

More and more companies—Hertz leading the way—now hold renters responsible for theft and vandalism if they don't buy the CDW. In response, some credit card and insurance companies are extending their coverage to rental cars. These include **Dreyfuss Bank Gold and Silver MasterCards** (tel. 800/847–9700), **Chase Manhattan Bank Visa Cards** (tel. 800/645–7352), and **Access America** (tel. 800/851–2800).

You should also find out before renting if you must pay for a full tank of gas whether you use it all or not. In addition, you should make sure the rental agency gives you a reservation number for the car you are planning to rent.

Staying in Waikiki

Important Addresses and Numbers

Hawaii Visitors Bureau 2270 Kalakaua Ave., 8th floor, Honolulu 96815, right in Waikiki, tel. 808/923–1811.

Emergencies 911 will get you the police, the fire department, an ambulance, or the suicide center.

Honolulu County Medical Society (tel. 808/536–6988)—information on doctors.

The Waikiki Drug Clinic (tel. 808/922–4787).

Coast Guard Rescue (tel. 808/536–4336).

Straub Walk-In Health Center. A doctor, laboratory/radiology technician, and nurses are on duty. No appointments are necessary. Services include diagnosis and treatment of illness and injury, laboratory testing and X-ray on site, and referral, when necessary, to Honolulu's Straub Hospital. More than 150 kinds of medical insurance are accepted, including Medicare, Medicaid, and most kinds of travel insurance. Sunburn care is a specialty. *Royal Hawaiian Shopping Center, 2233 Kalakaua*

*Ave., Bldg. B, 3rd floor, tel. 808/971–6000. Clinic open week-
days 8:30–5. At other times, call the duty doctor at 808/926–
4777.*

Hospitals **Straub Clinic,** 888 S. King St., Honolulu, tel. 808/522–4000;
Queen's Medical Center, 1301 Punchbowl St., Honolulu, tel.
808/547–4311; **Kapiolani Medical Center for Women and Children,** 1319 Punahou St., Honolulu, tel. 808/947–8633.

Pharmacies Both have the same ownership and advertise as sunburn spe-
cialists:

Outrigger Pharmacy (Outrigger Hotel, 2335 Kalakaua Ave.,
tel. 808/923–2529).
Kuhio Pharmacy (Outrigger West Hotel, 2330 Khuio Ave., tel.
923–4466).

Surf Report Dial 808/836–1952.

Weather Dial 808/836–0121.

Marine Forecast Dial 808/836–3921

Opening and Closing Times

Most Oahu banks are open Monday through Thursday 8:30–3 or
4:30, Fridays 8:30–6. Most financial institutions are closed on
weekends and holidays.

Major museums are open daily 9 or 10–4:30 or 5. The Honolulu
Academy of Arts is closed Sunday morning and all day Monday.
Most museums are closed on Christmas.

Major shopping malls are generally open daily 10–9, although
some shops may close at 4 or 5. Ala Moana Center is open weekdays 9:30–9, Saturday 9:30–5:30, Sunday 10–5.

Getting Around

Waikiki is only 2½ miles long and a half-mile wide. You can usually walk to where you are going. There are plenty of places to
stop and rest, the shop windows are interesting, and people-
watching is fun, and free.

Buses You can go all around the island or just down Kalakaua Avenue
for 60¢ on Honolulu's municipal transportation system, affec-
tionately known as The Bus (tel. 808/524–4626). You are also
entitled to one free transfer per fare if you ask for it when
boarding. Board at the front of the bus. Exact change is required. The student fare (grades 1–12) is 25¢ and children under 6 ride free. A free bus pass for senior citizens (age 65 or over
and able to prove it) may be obtained by applying in person at
725 Kapiolani Blvd. between 8 AM and 4 PM. Processing the free
senior pass used to require three weeks but now is completed
on a same-day basis. Monthly bus passes are available at $15 for
adults, $7.50 for students. In Waikiki, get them at Pioneer Fed-
eral Savings Bank, Waikiki Business Plaza, 2270 Kalakaua
Ave.

There are no official bus-route maps, but you can find privately
published booklets at most drugstores and other convenience
outlets. The important route numbers for Waikiki are 2, 4, 5, 8,
19, and 20. If you venture afield, you can always get back on one
of those.

There are also a number of brightly painted private buses, many free, that will take you to commercial attractions such as dinner cruises, garment factories, and the like.

Waikiki Trolley An open trolley cruises Waikiki, the Ala Moana area, and downtown, making 27 stops along a 90-minute route. The trolley ride provides a good orientation. The conductor narrates, pointing out sights, as well as shopping, dining, and entertainment opportunities along the way. *Tel. 808/526-0112. Buy an all-day pass from the conductor for $10 and for children under 12, $7. Daily 9 AM–5:45 PM.*

Taxis You can usually get one right at the doorstep of your hotel. Most restaurants will call a taxi for you. Rates are $1.75 at the drop of the flag, plus 25¢ for each additional ⅛ mile. Drivers are generally courteous and the cars in good condition, many of them air-conditioned. The two biggest taxicab companies are **Charley's,** a fleet of company-owned cabs (tel. 808/531–1333); and **SIDA of Hawaii, Inc.,** an association of individually owned cabs (tel. 808/836–0011).

Driving Your Mainland driver's license is valid in Hawaii for 90 days. If you're staying longer, apply for a Hawaii driver's license for $3 at the Honolulu Police Dept. Main Station, 1455 S. Beretania St., tel. 808/943–3111.

Be sure to buckle up. Hawaii has a seat-belt law for front-seat passengers. Children under age 3 must be in a car seat, available from your car-rental agency.

It's hard to get lost in Hawaii. Roads and streets, although they may be unpronounceable to the visitor (Kalanianaole Hwy., for example), are at least well marked. Major attractions and scenic spots are marked by the distinctive Hawaii Visitors Bureau sign with its red-caped warrior.

You can usually orient yourself by the mountains and the ocean. North, south, east, and west are less important than the local references. Go **mauka** means to go *toward the mountains* (north from Waikiki); go **makai** means to go *toward the ocean* (south); go toward **Diamond Head** means to go *in the direction of that famous landmark* (east); and go **ewa** (pronounced eva) means to go *away from Diamond Head* (west). You may be told that a shop is on the mauka–Diamond Head corner of the street, meaning it is on the mountain side of the street on the corner closest to Diamond Head. When giving directions, most local people state the highways by name, not by number.

Hawaii's drivers are generally courteous, and you rarely hear a horn. People will slow down and let you into traffic with a wave of the hand. A friendly wave back is appreciated and customary.

Driving in rush-hour traffic (6:30–8:30 AM and 3:30–5:30 PM) can be frustrating, not only because of the sheer volume of traffic but because left turns are forbidden at many intersections. Parking along many streets is curtailed during these hours, and towing is strictly enforced. Read the curbside parking signs before leaving your vehicle, even at a meter.

Don't leave valuables in your car. Tourists are targets for thieves because they probably won't be here by the time the case comes to trial, even if the crooks are caught.

Limos **Roberts Hawaii** (tel. 808/973–2308) has Cadillacs for $55 an hour. **Silver Cloud Limousine Service** (tel. 808/524–7999) will provide red-carpet treatment in its chauffeur-driven Rolls Royce limousines. Riding in such style costs $60 an hour with a two-hour minimum service required.

Mopeds and **Aloha Funway** (tel. 808/942–9696) has mopeds for $20–$24.95 a
Motorcycles day. Bicycles run from $12.95 a day.

Pedicabs You may have heard about them, but they have been banned, and no longer operate on the main streets. You may still find some cruising the side streets. Be sure to settle on the fare ahead of time, and don't buy anything else from the operator.

Guided Tours

Types of Tours **Circle Island Tour.** There are several variations on this theme. Read Scenic Drives around Oahu in the Excursions from Waikiki chapter to decide what's important to you and then see which tour comes the closest to matching your desires. Some of these all-day tours include lunch. Cost: $35–$45, depending on whether lunch is included or whether you go by bus or minibus, the latter being slightly more expensive.

Little Circle Tour. These tours cover the territory discussed in the East Oahu Ring section of Scenic Drives around Oahu in the Excursions from Waikiki chapter. Most of these tours are the same, no matter what the company. This is a half-day tour. Cost: about $20.

Pearl Harbor, City and Punchbowl Tour. This comprehensive tour includes the boat tour to Pearl Harbor run by the National Park Service. (*See* Tour 4: Circle Island Driving Tour in Chapter 4 for particulars on the attractions.) Cost: about $20.

Polynesian Cultural Center. *See* Chapter 4 for details on the center. The only advantage of the tour is that you don't have to drive yourself back to Waikiki after dark if you take in the evening show. Cost: about $50–$60.

Tour Companies Many "ground" companies handle these excursions. Some herd you onto an air-conditioned bus and others use smaller vans. Vans are recommended because less time is spent picking up passengers and you get to know your fellow passengers and your tour guide. Whether you go by bus or van, you'll probably be touring in top-of-the-line equipment. The competition among these companies is fierce, and everyone has to keep up. If you're booking through your hotel travel desk, ask whether you'll be on a bus or a van and exactly what the tour includes in the way of actual "get-off-the-bus" stops and "window sights."

Most of the tour guides have been in the business for years. Many have taken special Hawaiiana classes to learn their history and lore. They expect a tip ($1 per person at least), but they're just as cordial without one.

There are many tour companies. Here are some of the most reliable and popular:

American Express (tel. 808/924–6555). American Express books through several tour companies and can help you choose which tour best suits your needs.
Diamond Head Tours (tel. 808/922–0544). Guides must complete the Bishop Museum's Hawaiiana classes.

E Noa Tours (tel. 808/599–2561). This company uses vans exclusively and likes to get you into the outdoors. On one of its Circle Island Tours you get to swim at Hanauma Bay.

Polynesian Adventure Tours (tel. 808/922–0888). Some tours are action-oriented.

Roberts Hawaii (tel. 808/947–3939).

Trans Hawaiian Services (tel. 808/735–6467 or 800/533–8765). Guide "Uncle Joe" Kalahiki is considered by both tourism professionals and returning visitors to be the king of guides.

Walking Tours **Chinatown Walking Tour.** Meet at the Chinese Chamber of Commerce (42 N. King St.) for a fascinating peek into herbal shops, an acupuncturist's office, and specialty stores. The tour is sponsored by the Chinese Chamber of Commerce. Reservations required. *Tel. 808/533–3181. Cost: $4; add $5 to include lunch in a Chinese restaurant. Tues. only.*

"Historic Downtown Walking Tour." Volunteers from the Mission Houses Museum (553 S. King St.) take you on a two-hour walk through Honolulu, where the historic sites are side by side with the modern business towers. If it's Friday, end the tour by picking up a fast-food lunch and enjoying the noontime concert on the Iolani Palace lawn. *Tel. 808/531–0481. Reservations required. Cost: $7. Open weekdays.*

Clean Air Walks. Volunteers from this environmental action group conduct a variety of interesting walks, such as the "Wealthy Neighborhood Walk," the "Ala Moana Waterfront Walk," and a Diamond Head summit hike. Call for schedule. *Tel. 808/944–0804. Donation: $3–$5 to the Clean Air Fund. Fri. 9 AM.*

Great Outdoor Tours **Action Hawaii Adventures.** This company manages to compress into one day adventures the tourist rarely gets to do in a week. You'll go on guided hikes through rain forests and valleys, swim beneath waterfalls, and snorkel at "insider" spots. Boogieboarding and spearfishing are also available. A sandwich lunch plus samples of local food are included in the all-day tours. *Tel. 808/944–6754. Cost: $79.*

Helicopter Tours **Papillon.** People always think of helicopter rides as expensive, and they can be. But if you've never tried the whirlybird, this company has a 10- to 12-minute bird's-eye introductory view of Waikiki and Diamond Head for $45. The 30-minute flight for $99 through the Nuuanu Pali is beautiful, or you can circle the island for one hour for $187. One tour even goes to Molokai for lunch. Called the Oahu–Molokai Odyssey, it costs $275. Best of all, these helicopters take off from a pad right by the Ilikai, so you don't have to bother with the confusion of airport traffic. *Discovery Bay, 1778 Ala Moana Blvd., tel. 808/836–1566.*

Flightseeing Tours Several air tour companies offer the chance to see Hawaii from the skies. Even if your itinerary does not include stays on the Neighbor Islands, a flightseeing tour can give you an overview, so to speak, of the entire Aloha State. **Panorama Air Tour** offers a full-day, eight-island tour from Honolulu, with stops on the Big Island, Maui, and Kauai. Trips are made aboard twin-engine Piper Chieftains and cost $260. *100 Kalele Pl., Honolulu International Airport, tel. 808/836–2122 or 800/367–2671.*

Scenic Air Tours Hawaii, flying 10-passenger, twin-engine Beechcrafts, runs a similar route for $195. *100 Iolana Pl., Honolulu International Airport, tel. 800/352–3722 or 836–0044.*

2 Portraits of Waikiki

Hawaii at a Glance: A Chronology

c. AD 500 First human beings set foot on Hawaiian shores: Polynesians travel 2,000 miles in 60- to 80-foot canoes to the islands they name *Havaiki*, after their legendary homeland.

c. 1750 Birth of King Kamehameha.

1778 January: HMS *Resolution* and *Discovery*, captained by James Cook, land on Kauai; first Western encounter with Hawaii, which was not on any known Western map. Cook names the islands the Sandwich Islands after his patron, the Earl of Sandwich. November: Cook returns to Hawaii for the winter, anchors at Kealakekua Bay, on the Big Island.

1779 February: Cook is killed in a battle with indigenous people.

1786 Fur traders spend the winter in Hawaii; this becomes commonplace. Kamehameha consolidates his rule over the Big Island and attempts to extend his power over the other islands.

1790 First Westerners settle on islands.

1791 Kamehameha builds Puukohola Heiau temple; dedicates it by killing a rival chief.

1794 Kamehameha uses Western arms to complete his conquest of the islands.

1810 Chief of Kauai acknowledges Kamehameha's rule, uniting the islands under one chief.

1819 Death of Kamehameha; first whaling ships land at Lahaina on Maui.

1820 First missionaries arrive from Boston.

1835 First commercial sugar plantation on Kauai, financed by Americans.

1840 The Wilkes Expedition, sponsored by the U.S. Coast and Geodetic Survey, pinpoints Pearl Harbor as a potential naval base.

1852 Depopulation owing to Western diseases creates labor shortage; Chinese laborers brought in to work cane fields. They are followed by Portuguese, Japanese, Koreans, and Filipinos.

1863 Queen Emma, half-Caucasian widow of King Kamehameha IV, attempts to succeed her husband to the throne, but the Hawaiian legislature elects Chief David Kalakaua king.

1875 Treaty with United States establishes virtual protectorate, gives sugar planters trade protection.

1882 King David Kalakaua builds Iolani Palace on the site of the previous royal palace, after a visit to the United States.

1887 Treaty with United States renewed; grants United States exclusive use of Pearl Harbor.

1891–93 Reign of Queen Liliuokalani. She is removed from throne by American business interests led by Sanford B. Dole (son of a missionary), and imprisoned in Iolani Palace.

1898 Hawaii annexed by United States.

1900 Pineapple becomes a profitable crop.

1901 First major tourist hotel, the Moana (now called the Sheraton Moana Surfrider), built on Waikiki Beach.

1907 Fort Shafter Army Base built; first U.S. military post.

1908 Construction of base begins at Pearl Harbor.

1919 Pearl Harbor dedicated.

1927 Matson Navigation Company builds Royal Hawaiian Hotel as destination for its cruise ships.

1941 Pearl Harbor bombed by Japanese, causing United States to enter World War II.

1942 James Jones, with thousands of others, trains at Schofield Barracks on Oahu. He later writes about it in *From Here to Eternity*.

1959 Hawaii granted statehood. Later in the year, the first Boeing 707 jets make the flight from San Francisco in five hours; tourism greatly increases, becoming Hawaii's major industry.

Diamond Head Inside Out

by Betty
Fullard-Leo

A Hawaii
resident since
1962, Betty
Fullard-Leo is
editor of Pacific
Art & Travel
magazine.
Previously she
wrote and edited
for ALOHA
magazine and for
the Aloha
Travelers'
Newsletter.

The trail inside Diamond Head ambles off sedately enough from a green oasis irrigated into existence for Diamond Head State Park. It is later that the Sunday hiker, after crossing the open space of an old military target range, climbing the switchbacks, and blindly navigating a long, dark tunnel, becomes aware of a brooding sense of history in the ancient lava walls of this famous landmark.

The going gets tougher, as well as more intriguing, with a climb up concrete steps at the end of the tunnel into a catacomb of concrete hallways and barred rooms. Knowledgeable hikers avoid the stairs by taking a gentle path at their base along the outer edge of the crater rim. The splendor of Oahu's southeast coastline is spread out in a buffet of vistas from atop a concrete bunker just below the summit.

Black Point, a spit of land that harbors some of Hawaii's most opulent homes, is easy to identify. The whale-shaped hump of land beyond is Koko Head Crater. Inland, the imposing horseshoe-shaped Koko Crater evokes images of the fiery origins of the Hawaiian Islands that burst from the sea in flames millions of years earlier.

The story of Diamond Head itself goes back to a catastrophic explosion that created the crater about 150,000 years ago, or perhaps the story begins even earlier when the lava peaks that form the Hawaiian chain edged their way above the surface of the ocean. Of the eight major islands, Kauai was the first to surface, four or five million years ago. With the movement of the great tectonic plates of land under the sea, it gradually drifted to the northwest. Oahu appeared next as two separate volcanos of different ages. The older Waianae Range is on the western side, while the younger Koolau Range that separates the windward and leeward sides of Oahu is some two-and-a-half million years old. Lava flows from the Koolau volcano spilled into the sea to form the central plateau that today connects the two mountain ranges of Oahu.

In geologic times, a group of thirty relatively recent eruptions called the Honolulu Volcanic Series created the most obvious landmarks around Honolulu. These are the cinder cones and craters of Punchbowl National Cemetery, Diamond Head, Hanauma Bay, Rabbit Island, and Koko Crater, among others.

Diamond Head is a tuff cone, a type of volcano formed when molten rock, working its way toward the surface of the earth, comes in contact with water-saturated rocks. Theor-

"Diamond Head Inside Out" first appeared in ALOHA, The Magazine of Hawaii and the Pacific. Reprinted with permission from Davick Publications.

ies vary, but most geologists agree that about 150,000 years ago, Diamond Head burst into being in an explosion that sprayed fine brown ash and pulverized rock and coral up to two miles in the air. Northeast tradewinds blew the settling ash southwest to create Leahi Peak, ringed by a nearly perfect conical crater with an average height of 400 feet. Geologists theorize erosion has carved away as much as a quarter of a mile on Diamond Head's seaward side. To prevent further erosion inside the crater, signs warn today's hikers to stay on the trail, but it is in these eroded areas that the bits of white coral and brown ash that are compacted to layers of rock in the walls of the crater are visible.

Because of this erosion, calcite crystals commonly known as "Pele's tears" once lay about the base, causing British sailors to christen the volcano "Diamond" Head in the 19th century. The Hawaiians had always called it "Laeahi" or "Leahi," possibly reflecting their early practice of lighting signal fires on the summit to guide home their fishing canoes. "Lae" means headland while "ahi" means fire. Another popular explanation for the Hawaiian name interprets "lae" as forehead, while "ahi" means tuna. Glance at any yellow-fin tuna in the fishmarket, and the similarity between Diamond Head's familiar profile and that of the tuna is obvious. It was given its first English name in 1786 when Captain Nathaniel Portlock called it Point Rose in honor of the secretary of the British treasury, but the name didn't stick. At other times it was dubbed Diamond Hill and Conical Mountain.

Hawaiians had their own explanation for the formation of Diamond Head. They believed the fire goddess, Pele, and her sister, Hiiaka, were driven from their home by an older jealous sister, Namakaokahai. The two goddesses went to live first on Kauai, causing the eruption of Puu Ka Pele as evidence of their presence. Namakaokahai drove them to Oahu, but the sea put out their fire at Leahi, so they moved on to Molokai, to Maui, and finally came to reside on the Big Island of Hawaii, where Pele continues to show her spirit-presence in eruptions at Kilauea Volcano.

Diamond Head was a sacred mountain to the Hawaiians, who once had five heiaus, or places of worship, in the crater. The stone remains of only one still exist. Kapua Heiau and Kupalaha Heiau were near Kapiolani Park. Fragments of a remaining wall show Kapua Heiau was approximately 240 feet square. Two heiaus had special purposes. Ahi Heiau on the peak of Diamond Head was a shrine dedicated to the god of winds. It served as protection against the updrafts that might put out the guiding light. Pahu-a-Manu Heiau was specifically for fishermen and seamen. Located where today's lighthouse stands, the men could watch for schools of fish while their priests made offerings at the site.

The most important heiau was Papaenaena, which was visible from Waikiki during the 19th century. Located approximately where the Hawaii School for Girls now stands, it is thought to have been built by the Maui king Kahekili to commemorate his conquest of Oahu and to execute the king of Oahu on a heiau that hadn't been used for the execution of one of his own ancestors. Papaenaena Heiau was dedicated to the war god Kukailimoku. It was here that King Kamehameha the Great celebrated his victory over Kalanikupule, the king of Oahu, Maui, Molokai, and Lanai, after the battle at Nuunau Pali in 1795. The heiau again figured in history in 1804 when Kamehameha lost his battle to conquer Kauai. Temple priests recommended a 10-day tabu and sacrificed 400 pigs, 400 coconuts, 400 branches of plantains and three human victims to appease the gods.

An early visitor to the Islands, John B. Whitman, wrote of his visit to Papaenaena in 1814: "I watched an opportunity to enter it and perceived a quantity of bones and cocoa nut shells scattered about, and on one side there was a pile of human skulls reaching half way to the top of the wall. I afterwards learned the skulls and bones were the remains of victims sacrificed to the Etour (gods). The walls of this charnel house were decorated with skulls placed along the top at intervals of a foot with the face outward as if to warn the unwary of their doom if their feet encroached upon the sacred spot."

Upon the death of Kamehameha in 1819 and the destruction of the religious kapu system by his heirs, the heiaus were abandoned or destroyed.

Papaenaena's three terraces were demolished in 1856, and its stones were used for fencing and roadwork. Some of these paving stones still remain around Iolani Palace.

The next 40 years were a relatively quiet time in Diamond Head's history. Horses grazed among the scrub brush in the interior. An alkaline sink covered a portion of the 175-acre floor. A few private homes were built beneath its slopes on the Waikiki side, and in the early 1890s, the first steel-frame lighthouse was constructed on the seaward side. This was replaced and equipped with the latest automatic electric equipment 27 years later.

The political climate in Hawaii deteriorated into turmoil, and on January 7, 1893, a group of annexationists, led by Honolulu's American population, took control of the principal government buildings. They proclaimed a provisional government and deposed the queen. By January 6, 1895, native rebels or royalists, who were dissatisfied with the new government and who felt that Queen Liliuokalani should be returned to her rightful position as ruler, staged a rebellion that included "The Battle of Diamond Head."

The royalists were armed with 288 repeating Winchester rifles and 100 pistols that had been ordered from San Francisco. On the afternoon of January 6, Sam Nowlein, commander of the household troops under Liliuokalani, gave word that rebels should assemble at Diamond Head at 2 AM the next morning, but some of the rebels misunderstood the order and began to assemble immediately. When the government forces realized what was happening, martial law was declared and the National Guard and Citizens' Guard organizations were called to duty. Company E of the National Guard went to quell the 150 armed men mobilizing on the slopes of Diamond Head. Robert Wilcox, their leader, ordered his men to retreat to a better position on the rim of the crater, and fighting commenced.

At the same time, Sam Nowlein was leading another group of rebels in a battle at Moiliili. Fighting at Diamond Head went on during the day but as night fell, the royalists under Wilcox fled to Manoa Valley. Within a week, all of the royalists had been captured and Queen Liliuokalani was arrested and placed in confinement. Before a special military commission 190 prisoners were tried; only six were acquitted. Some were sentenced to be executed, others to prison terms and fines, but Sanford Dole, president of the Republic of Hawaii, later reduced most of the sentences as being too severe. Even the revised sentences were never carried out and by the time the United States annexed the Islands in 1898, all the prisoners had been pardoned.

In 1904 the United States government bought 729 acres around the crater for $3,300 at the recommendation of Major William E. Birkhimer. Assuming it could be found, a 100,000-square-foot lot for sale on Diamond Head today (granted it would probably have a house on it) might run anywhere from $350,000 to more than $1,000,000.

For 44 years the military closed Diamond Head crater to the public. Bunkers, gun mounts, battery and storage tunnels, observation posts, and communications rooms were constructed prior to World War II. A cable car lifted men and supplies from the crater floor to the west wall. During the war years, hundreds of soldiers occupied barracks in the crater. The existing trail was built between 1908 and 1910, but in the 1940s, camouflage nets hung like giant spider webs from high metal posts to hide traffic on the trail from curious eyes. Activities inside the crater were classified information.

Hikers in the crater today can still see the metal posts along the trail and can enter the concrete "lookouts" for sightseeing on five levels. Each level commands a different view of Oahu's coastline from the lowest "Station Able," with its windows focused southeast, to the top "Station Easy," which looks to the west toward Pearl Harbor. It's only a short walk up a more recently installed metal staircase to the 763-foot Leahi summit. Swimming pools shine like giant blue sapphires in the Diamond Head residential area below, the pink Royal Hawaiian Hotel is dwarfed by

Waikiki's high rises, and, farther up the coast to the west are the concrete ribbons that are Honolulu Airport's reef runway shimmering in the heat. Beyond is Pearl Harbor. The view is spectacular.

The return hike wends through a series of stairways and halls that connect the five lookout stations. A feeling of history and secrecy brings to mind the years when Diamond Head, with its fortifications, was known as the "Gibraltar of the Pacific." These underground rooms have prison-like bars, not because they housed fugitives, but because they held secret codes that had to remain under lock and key. The bars allowed air to circulate better than solid walls and doors.

The guns on Diamond Head were never used in war, and in 1950 the Army removed its paraphernalia and turned its facilities over to the Hawaii National Guard. Birkhimer Tunnel, a 14,728-square-foot room dug into the northeastern side of the crater, is used today by Hawaii's Civil Defense organization.

In 1955 and 1958 the Territory of Hawaii and the Federal Aviation Agency were given the land for defense and for air traffic control. A two-story green building in the crater now houses the FAA Center which directs the flight of approaching and departing planes when they are not in contact with the tower at the Honolulu International Airport.

Diamond Head was designated a national monument in 1968. Since then, it has attracted more and more visitors, even though tour operators are not allowed to conduct tours in Hawaii's public parks. Whatever the future holds for Diamond Head, it's a good bet that in some form it will stand sentinel over Hawaii's history and the resort area of Waikiki for years to come.

The Aloha Shirt: A Colorful Swatch of Island History

by DeSoto Brown

A fourth-generation Islander of part-Hawaiian ancestry, DeSoto Brown is the author of two books, Hawaii Recalls *and* Aloha Waikiki.

Elvis Presley had an entire wardrobe of them in the '60s films *Blue Hawaii* and *Paradise, Hawaiian Style*. During the '50s, entertainer Arthur Godfrey and bandleader Harry Owens often sported them on television shows. John Wayne loved to lounge around in them. Mick Jagger felt compelled to buy one on a visit to Hawaii in the 1970s. Dustin Hoffman, Steven Spielberg and Bill Cosby avidly collect them.

From gaudy to grand, from tawdry to tasteful, aloha shirts are Hawaii's gift to the world of fashion. It's been more than 50 years since those riotously colored garments made their first appearance as immediately recognizable symbols of the Islands.

The roots of the aloha shirt go back to the early 1930s, when Hawaii's garment industry was just beginning to develop its own unique style. Although locally made clothes did exist, they were almost exclusively items for plantation workers, which were constructed of durable palaka or plain cotton material.

Out of this came the first stirrings of fashion: Beachboys and schoolchildren started having sport shirts made from colorful Japanese kimono fabric. The favored type of cloth was the kind used for children's kimonos—bright pink and orange floral prints for girls; masculine motifs in browns and blues for boys. In Japan, such flamboyant patterns were considered unsuitable for adult clothing, but in the Islands, such rules didn't apply, and it seemed the flashier the shirt, the better—for either sex. Thus, the aloha shirt was born.

It was easy and inexpensive in those days to have garments tailored to order; the next step was moving to mass production and marketing. In June 1935, Honolulu's best-known tailoring establishment, Musa-Shiya, advertised the availability of "Aloha shirts—well tailored, beautiful designs and radiant colors. Ready-made or made to order . . . 95¢ and up." This is the first known printed use of the term that would soon refer to an entire industry. By the following year, several local manufacturers had begun full-scale production of "aloha wear." One of them, Ellery Chun of King-Smith, registered as local trademarks the terms "Aloha

"The Aloha Shirt: A Colorful Swatch of Island History" first appeared in ALOHA, The Magazine of Hawaii and the Pacific. *Reprinted with permission of Davick Publications.*

Sportswear" and "Aloha Shirt" in 1936 and 1937, respectively.

These early entrepreneurs were the first to create uniquely Hawaiian designs for fabric as well—splashy patterns that would forever symbolize the Islands. A 1939 *Honolulu Advertiser* story described them as a "delightful confusion (of) tropical fish and palm trees, Diamond Head and the Aloha Tower, surfboards and leis, ukuleles and Waikiki beach scenes."

The aloha wear of the late 1930s was intended for—and mostly worn by—tourists, and interestingly, a great deal of it was exported to the Mainland and even Europe and Australia. By the end of the decade, for example, only 5% of the output of one local firm, the Kamehameha Garment Company, was sold in Hawaii.

World War II brought this trend to a halt, and during the postwar period, aloha wear really came into its own in Hawaii. A strong push to support local industry gradually nudged Island garb into the workplace, and kamaainas began to wear the clothing that previously had been seen as attire for visitors.

In 1947, for example, male employees of the City and County of Honolulu were first allowed to wear aloha shirts "in plain shades" during the summer months. Later that year, the first observance of Aloha Week started the tradition of "bankers and bellhops . . . mix(ing) colorfully in multi-hued and tapa-designed Aloha shirts every day," as a local newspaper's Sunday magazine supplement noted in 1948. By the 1960s, "Aloha Friday," set aside specifically for the wearing of aloha attire, had become a tradition. In the following decade, the suit and tie practically disappeared as work attire in Hawaii, even for executives.

Most of the Hawaiian-themed fabric used in manufacturing aloha wear was designed in the Islands, then printed on the Mainland or in Japan. The glowingly vibrant rayons of the late '40s and early '50s (a period now seen as aloha wear's heyday) were at first printed on the East Coast, but manufacturers there usually required such large orders, local firms eventually found it impossible to continue using them. By 1964, 90% of Hawaiian fabric was being manufactured in Japan—a situation that still exists today.

Fashion trends usually move in cycles, and aloha wear is no exception. By the 1960s, the "chop suey print" with its "tired clichés of Diamond Head, Aloha Tower, outrigger canoes (and) stereotyped leis" was seen as corny and garish, according to an article published in the *Honolulu Star-Bulletin*. But it was just that outdated aspect that began to appeal to the younger crowd, who began searching out old-fashioned aloha shirts at the Salvation Army and Goodwill thrift stores. These shirts were dubbed "silkies," a name by which they're still known, even though most of them were actually made of rayon.

Before long, what had been 50-cent shirts began escalating in price, and a customer who had balked at paying $5 for a shirt that someone had already worn soon found the same item selling for $10—and more. By the late 1970s, aloha wear designers were copying the prints of yesteryear for their new creations.

The days of bargain silkies are now gone. The few choice aloha shirts from decades past that still remain are offered today by specialized dealers for hundreds of dollars apiece, causing many to look back with chagrin to the time when such treasures were foolishly worn to the beach until they fell apart. The best examples of vintage aloha shirts are now rightly seen as art objects worthy of preservation for the lovely depictions they offer of Hawaii's colorful and unique scene.

Hawaii's History

Hawaii's chain of volcanic islands, blessed by sunshine, soft winds, and jagged green mountains, rises out of a lonely stretch of the North Pacific, thousands of miles from land. No one knows exactly when these islands were first inhabited. Although it was originally believed that the first people arrived in the 11th century, new evidence indicates that they arrived about 500 years earlier.

The exact identification of these first settlers is also unclear. Most researchers believe they were people originally from Southeast Asia who discovered the South Pacific islands of Tahiti and the Marquesas. The most prevalent theory is that they probably came from the Marquesas, now part of French Polynesia. Why they ended up in Hawaii is open to debate.

One thing is certain: This string of islands was settled by seafaring people whose seamanship had already taken them to many islands in the vast southern and eastern expanses of the Pacific. The staggering proportions of their feats can be fully appreciated only if one considers that they sailed across 2,000 miles of open ocean centuries before the Vikings left Europe's shores and more than 1,000 years before the first voyage of Columbus. It's not even known what these people called themselves. The original inhabitants of Hawaii were named Polynesians by Europeans. Polynesia means "many islands" in Greek and refers to the oceanic realm of the South Pacific.

If settlers did indeed first set foot on Hawaii in the 6th century, it would be nearly 1,300 years later before the first European laid eyes on these islands. Captain James Cook, an Englishman, first sighted the island of Oahu on January 18, 1778, and "discovered" it for the Western world.

Captain Cook, commander of the HMS *Resolution* and the consort vessel HMS *Discovery*, was already known as England's greatest explorer of the world's uncharted oceans. Cook had discovered dozens of South Pacific islands on two previous voyages. On his third venture into the Pacific, he was going north of the equator into the uncharted North Pacific, in search of the legendary Northwest Passage, believed to be a seaway link between the Pacific and the Atlantic. After spending Christmas Day on an atoll north of Tahiti, which he named Christmas Island, he set sail for the top of the North American continent. He did not expect to see land again until he had crossed nearly 3,000 miles of ocean.

But just 16 days later, Cook and all hands were on deck, gazing in wonder as they saw the mountains of the Hawaiian Islands looming in the distance through the predawn mist. They were even more astonished when they saw people in canoes rowing toward them from the shore.

Cook stepped ashore onto the island of Kauai, the first of the Islands he was to visit. He named the archipelago the Sandwich Islands, for the Earl of Sandwich, his patron. In 1779 Cook was killed in a fight with Hawaiians at Kealakekua on the island of Hawaii.

The splendid isolation of the Islands ended abruptly after Cook's arrival. First came British explorers, then came British, American, French, and Russian traders. Whalers from New England soon followed. Tales spread of thousands of acres of sugarcane growing wild, and the farmers came in droves, from the United States and Europe.

At the time of Cook's arrival, each island was ruled as an independent kingdom by hereditary chiefs, who often warred among themselves. One such chief was Kamehameha, who was the first to unify the Islands. He began his rise to power in 1790 through a series of bloody battles to unify the island of Hawaii. He then went on to conquer Maui and Oahu. By the time of his death in 1819, he was King Kamehameha I, ruling the unified Kingdom of Hawaii with an iron hand. Hawaii had a total of seven monarchs, four of them descendants of Kamehameha I. The Islands would remain a monarchy until 1893, when Queen Liliuokalani, the last of Hawaii's monarchs, was deposed during a bloodless revolution that led to a provisional government headed by an American, Sanford Ballard Dole. He proclaimed himself president of the Republic of Hawaii in 1894.

One of the pivotal years in Hawaiian history was 1820, the year the first missionaries arrived from New England. At this time, King Kamehameha I had only been dead one year, yet already the social order was beginning to break down. The Hawaiians were disillusioned with their own gods and were receptive to the ideas of Christianity. The influx of Western culture had also brought the introduction of Western diseases, liquor, and what some viewed as moral decay. The missionaries gained great success because they aligned themselves with the chiefs against some of the evils linked to the Westerners.

The second king to reign was Kamehameha II, the eldest of two sons of the first king. His short reign was noted for the official demise of the pagan religion, which included human sacrifice, and the breakdown of ancient taboos, such as the taboo against women eating with men, something which for centuries had been punishable by death. King Kamehameha II and his queen died of measles in 1824.

His younger brother became King Kamehameha III, a wise and gentle sovereign who ruled for 30 years. King Kamehameha III turned Hawaii into a constitutional monarchy in 1849, and won official recognition of Hawaii as an independent country by the United States, France, and Great Britain. In 1845 the King and the Legislature moved the seat of government from Lahaina, on Maui, to Honolulu, on Oahu. His other many notable accomplishments include the opening of Maui's Lahainaluna School, the oldest high school west of the Rocky Mountains; the establishment of the first permanent sugar plantation; and the publication of the first newspaper in the Pacific area.

In the early 1850s, toward the end of King Kamehameha III's reign, Hawaii's legendary ethnic diversity began in earnest, driven by labor shortages in the sugarcane fields. Between 1852 and 1946 a steady stream of foreign labor poured into Hawaii. The first to arrive were the Chinese, brought in by contract, to work on the sugarcane plantations. The Japanese began arriving in 1868, and later came Filipinos, Koreans, Portuguese, and Puerto Ricans.

The importance of sugar in Hawaii's political and economic history cannot be overstated. American merchants in Honolulu financed the first commercial sugar plantation on Kauai in 1835. Plantations soon sprouted on Oahu, Maui, and the island of Hawaii. By the end of the 19th century, sugar was "king" and Hawaii's only major export. As the importance of sugar in the local economy grew, the plantation owners began looking toward annexation with the United States as a means of establishing a firm market for their product. But the monarchs did not support annexation.

Kamehameha IV and V, grandsons of the first king, ruled about eight years each. With the death in 1872 of Kamehameha V, the line of direct descendents of the first king ended. A series of power struggles ensued between the adherents of David Kalakaua, who was elected by the Hawaii Legislature, and supporters of the Dowager Queen Emma, widow of Kamehameha IV. American and British marines were called in to restore order.

King Kalakaua reigned from 1874 through 1891, a turbulent period in which he battled for an increase in the personal authority of the king and dreamed of a Polynesian empire. It was during his reign that the United States and Hawaii signed a treaty of reciprocity in 1875, assuring Hawaii a duty-free market for sugar in the United States. The treaty's renewal in 1887 gave the United States the exclusive use of Pearl Harbor as a coaling station. Hawaii's strategic importance as a naval base was recognized as early as 1840 when the first U.S. survey of the Hawaiian Islands singled out Pearl Harbor as having enormous potential for harboring warships.

King Kalakaua, who died in 1891 during a visit to San Francisco, was succeeded by his sister, Liliuokalani, the last monarch of Hawaii. She unwittingly opened the door to efforts of the sugar barons to annex Hawaii to the United States. In trying to eliminate the restrictions that had been placed on the monarchy, Queen Liliuokalani brought on a bloodless revolution and was deposed after reigning only two years.

Sanford Ballard Dole, who formed a provisional government, requested Hawaii's annexation by the United States, but President Grover Cleveland refused. As a result, the provisional government converted Hawaii into a republic and proclaimed Dole president in 1894. The outbreak of the Spanish-American War in 1898 and Hawaii's strategic military importance in the Pacific led the next U.S. president, William McKinley, to look toward annexation with a more sympathetic eye. On August 12, 1898, Hawaii was officially annexed, by a joint resolution of Congress. Sanford Dole was appointed first governor of the territory on February 20, 1901.

A cousin of Sanford Dole, James D. Dole, developed the pineapple industry in Hawaii. This cousin was a New Englander who experimented with pineapples until he found a variety that would grow successfully in the Islands. In 1903 he made his first canned pineapple pack, producing nearly 2,000 cases. This marked the beginning of Hawaii's great pineapple industry, which today is much more prominent than its sugar industry.

In the early 1900s, Hawaii's military industry also gained importance. In 1907 Fort Shafter, headquarters for the U.S. Army, became the first permanent military post in the Islands. Dredging of the channel at Pearl Harbor began in 1908. Formally dedicated by the U.S. Navy in 1919, Pearl Harbor would become a tragic part of U.S. history on December 7, 1941, when the U.S. Pacific Fleet was attacked by the Japanese. Nearly 4,000 casualties resulted from that surprise attack. Today, Pearl Harbor and the USS *Arizona* Memorial are among Hawaii's major tourist attractions.

In the 1920s Hawaiians began to increase efforts to promote tourism, the industry that would eventually dominate development of the Islands. In 1927 Army Lieutenants Lester Maitland and Albert Hegenberger made the first successful nonstop flight from the mainland. Commercial interisland air service began two years later. In 1936 Pan American World Airways made history as the first to start regular commercial passenger flights to Hawaii from the Mainland.

The year Hawaii gained statehood, 1959, was a major turning point in the history of the Islands for yet another reason: the first Boeing 707 jet planes arrived, flying from California to Honolulu in a record five hours. That same year, 243,216 tourists visited Hawaii. Today tourism is Hawaii's largest industry, drawing more than 6 million visitors a year.

While Hawaii's sugar, pineapple, military, and tourist industries were growing, the dream of statehood grew stronger. The campaign for statehood began at the turn of the century, with the overthrow of the last monarch. The road to statehood was a slow one, an acrimonious struggle taking more than half a century. Racism was blamed for many of the problems. Hawaii's great racial diversity did not sit well with some conservative members of Congress who resisted the idea of statehood for a territory that was heavily non-Caucasian. Anti-Japanese sentiment following the attack on Pearl Harbor further fueled the debate. But Hawaiians persevered, and on March 12, 1959, Congress passed legislation admitting Hawaii into the Union. Hawaii officially became the 50th state on Admission Day, August 21, 1959.

Hawaii's royal history may be rediscovered on Oahu, not far from Waikiki. The Iolani Palace, located in downtown Honolulu, is an elaborately restored, four-story Italian Renaissance structure, built in 1882 by the last Hawaiian king, David Kalakaua. It was here also that Queen Liliuokalani, the last reigning monarch, was deposed and imprisoned for nearly eight months by American businessmen who wanted Hawaii annexed to the United States.

Another royal treasure is Queen Emma Summer Palace, once the home of Kamehameha IV's wife. Now a museum, this estate recalls a history of misfortune that plagued Queen Emma, who, in her late twenties, suffered the death of her infant son Prince Albert and Kamehameha IV within 15 months of each other. She then tried and failed to succeed her husband to the throne.

Hawaii has been careful to preserve its past, especially its ancient history. Much of this past is found on the land itself rather than in old buildings; ancient burial caves, royal fish ponds, and petroglyph fields are likely to be found alongside of seaside resorts. State and federal laws have made archaeology in Hawaii a priority. An archaeological site investigation is required before any new construction can begin. This not only protects what already exists, but it has often led to new revelations about when the Islands were first inhabited.

3 Exploring Waikiki

Introduction

It's usually too sunny, too beautiful, and too warm to spend an entire day walking around Waikiki, no matter how interesting the sights may be. The three walks described here take you from one end of Waikiki to the other. You can try one walk a day sandwiched between time at the beach or you could do all three in one day. Some of the sights are a bit off the beaten track, not in terms of distance but in terms of what's been hyped.

Directions in the area are often given as:

mauka—toward the mountains (north); **makai**—toward the ocean (south); **Diamond Head**—toward Diamond Head (east); and **ewa**—away from Diamond Head (west).

You'll find these terms used in this chapter and the following chapter, Excursions from Waikiki.

Highlights for First-time Visitors

Army Museum, Tour 1
Damien Museum, Tour 2
Diamond Head, A Waikiki Hike
Honolulu Zoo, Tour 3
International Market Place, Tour 2
Kodak Hula Show, Tour 3
Kuhio Beach Park, Waikiki Beaches
Royal Hawaiian Hotel, Tour 1
Sheraton Moana Surfrider, Tour 2
Waikiki Aquarium, Tour 3

Tour 1

Numbers in the margin correspond with points of interest on the Waikiki map.

❶ The **Ilikai Waikiki Hotel** (1777 Ala Moana Blvd.) is a good place to start a walking tour. From the second-floor pool deck,
❷ there's a good view of the **Ala Wai Yacht Harbor,** home berth to an armada of pleasure boats and two yacht clubs, both of which are open to members only. America's Cup champion skipper Dennis Conner hung his binnacle at the Waikiki Yacht Club when training for his victorious race against the Australians in 1987. It's fun to ride the Ilikai Waikiki's glass elevator, but it doesn't start running until 5:30 PM. From Annabelle's lounge at the top, the views of the sunset are spectacular, and you can see the whole of Waikiki stretching toward Diamond Head.

❸ Head toward the main intersection of Ala Moana Boulevard and Kalia Road. Take a little detour to the **Rainbow Bazaar** shopping center in the **Hilton Hawaiian Village** (2005 Kalia Rd.). The Rainbow Bazaar is an elegant hodgepodge of Asian architecture, with a Chinese moon gate and pagoda and a Japanese farmhouse with a water wheel, all dominated by the tall mosaic mural of the Rainbow Tower. This is a good place to browse and pick up aloha shirts.

Stroll through the lavish gardens and look for the penguin pond in back of the main lobby. The hotel fronts the pretty Kahanamoku Lagoon and beach. It looks like the quintessential tropical lagoon, complete with a little island and palm trees.

4 Across the street on Kalia Road is the U.S. Army's **Fort DeRussy.** On Saturday evenings during the summer, there are Catholic Masses on the lawn by the beach, with the setting sun as a backdrop and a lot of Hawaiian pageantry as part of the service. (For the schedule, tel. 808/263–8844.) Battery Randolf (Building 32) was built in 1909 as a key in the defense of Pearl Harbor and Honolulu. Within its walls, which measure 22 feet thick in places, is the **Army Museum,** housing an intimidating collection of war paraphernalia. The major focus is World War II memorabilia, but exhibits range from ancient Hawaiian weaponry to displays relating to the Vietnam War. *Tel. 808/ 438–2821. Group guided tours can be arranged. Admission free. Open 10 AM–4:30 PM; closed Mon.*

5 Across the street from Fort DeRussy, at 245 Saratoga Rd., nestled snugly amid the commerce of Waikiki, is an oasis of tranquility: the **Tea House of the Urasenke Foundation.** Take part in a Japanese tea ceremony; you'll be served tea and sweets by ladies in kimonos. The Urasenke Foundation is a centuries-old institution based in Kyoto, Japan. It has set the etiquette for the tea ceremony based on the Zen philosophy that has influenced Japanese art and taste. The Waikiki teahouse was donated by the Kyoto foundation and was the first to be built outside Japan. The teahouse is a good, basic introduction to Japanese culture. Wear something comfortable (but no shorts, please) for sitting on the floor. *Tel. 808/923–3059. Open Wed. and Fri., 10 AM.* Minimum donation: $2.

6 With a little zip from the tea and a little Zen for the road, head mauka (toward the mountains, north) toward Kalakaua Avenue and turn toward Diamond Head. At **First Hawaiian Bank** (2181 Kalakaua Ave.) on the corner of Lewers Street, look in the lobby for six massive murals; these paintings depict the populating of Hawaii. They also deal with the evolution of Hawaiian culture—from Hawaiian arts before contact with the Western world to the introduction of the first printing press to the Islands in 1872. The impressive panels were painted by the late Jean Charlot, whose work is represented in the Uffizi Gallery in Florence, the British Museum in London, and the Metropolitan Museum and the Museum of Modern Art in New York. The murals are beautifully lit at night, with some panels visible from the street.

7 Across the street, at 2200 Kalakaua Avenue, is one of Waikiki's architectural landmarks, the blue-tile roof of the **Gump Building.** Built in 1929, it was once the premier store of Hawaii and was known for the quality of its Asian and Hawaiian objects. Now it houses a Crazy Shirts T-shirt shop and a McDonald's.

8 Walk down Lewers Street toward the ocean, to the impressive **Halekulani Hotel** (2199 Kalia Rd.). The most interesting thing about the hotel, aside from its famed restaurants, is the gigantic floral arrangement in the lobby. While you're there, take a peek at the swimming pool with its huge orchid mosaic at the bottom. Incorporated into the relatively new Halekulani Hotel is a portion of its old (1917) structure, which was the setting for the first of the Charlie Chan detective novels, *The House without a Key.*

Time Out If it's lunchtime, you should enjoy dining at **Orchids** restaurant in the Halekulani with a view of Diamond Head from every table. The lunch menu includes light entrées and tasty salads.

Waikiki

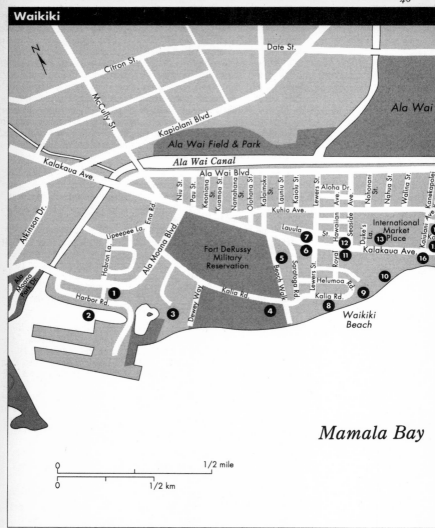

Citron St.

Date St.

McCully St.

Kapiolani Blvd.

Ala Wai Field & Park

Ala Wai

Kalakaua Ave.

Ala Wai Canal

Ala Wai Blvd.

Atkinson Dr.

Niu St.
Pau St.
Keoniana St.
Kuamoo St.
Namahana St.
Olohana St.
Kalaimoku St.
Launiu St.
Kaiolu St.
Lewers St.
Aloha Dr.
Ave.
Nohonani St.
Nahua St.
Walina St.
Kanekapolei

Kuhio Ave.

Lipeepee La.

Hobron La.

Ala Moana Blvd.

Ena Rd.

Lauula

7

6

Lavula St.

Hawaiian

Seaside

Duke's La.

12

Royal

Kalakaua Ave.

International
Market
Place

13

Kaiulani Ave.

Koa

Ala Moana Park Dr.

Fort DeRussy
Military
Reservation

Beach Walk

Saratoga Rd.

5

Lewers St.

11

Harbor Rd.

1

Dewey Way

Kalia Rd.

3

2

Helumoa Rd.

9

Kalia Rd.

8

4

10

16

Waikiki
Beach

Mamala Bay

0 ——————— 1/2 mile
0 ——————— 1/2 km

Ala Wai Yacht Harbor, **2**	Halekulani Hotel, **8**	Kahuna (or Wizard) Stones, **16**	Rainbow Bazaar Hilton Hawaiian Village, **3**
Damien Museum, **19**	Hawaii Visitors Bureau, **12**	Kapiolani Bandstand, **24**	Royal Hawaiian Hotel, **10**
Diamond Head, **28**	Hilton Hawaiian Village, **3**	Kapiolani Park, **21**	Royal Hawaiian Shopping Center, **11**
First Hawaiian Bank, **6**	Honolulu Zoo, **20**	Kapiolani Park Rose Garden, **27**	Saint Augustine's, **18**
Fort De Russy, **4**	Hyatt Regency Waikiki, **15**	King's Village, **14**	Sheraton Moana Surfrider, **16**
Gardens, Royal Hawaiian Hotel, **10**	Ilikai Waikiki Hotel, **1**	Kodak Hula Show, **23**	Sheraton Waikiki, **9**
Gump Building, **7**	International Market Place, **13**	Pacific Beach Hotel, **17**	

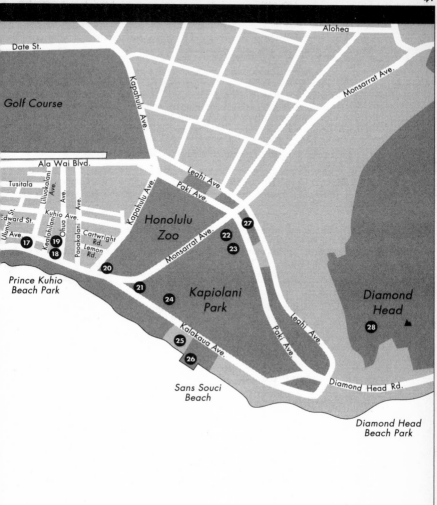

Golf Course

Date St.

Alohea

Monsarrat Ave.

Ala Wai Blvd.

Tusitala

Liliuokalani Ave.

Kealohilani Ave.

Ohua

Kuhio Ave.

Paoakalani

Edward St.

Uluniu Ave.

Kapahulu Ave.

Kapahulu Ave.

Cartwright Rd.

Lemon Rd.

Leahi Ave.

Paki Ave.

Honolulu Zoo

Monsarrat Ave.

Prince Kuhio Beach Park

Kapiolani Park

Kalakaua Ave.

Sans Souci Beach

Paki Ave.

Leahi Ave.

Diamond Head Rd.

Diamond Head

Diamond Head Beach Park

17 18 19 20 21 22 23 24 25 26 27 28

Tea House of the
Urasenke
Foundation, **5**
Waikiki Aquarium, **25**
Waikiki Business
Plaza, **12**
Waikiki Shell, **22**
Waikiki War Memorial
Natatorium, **26**
Zoo Fence Art
Mart, **20**

But if you're looking for eye-boggling quantity, wait a few minutes until you reach the **Royal Hawaiian Hotel** and try its famous lunch buffet in the Surf Room, $15.75, served daily noon–2:30 PM.

From the Halekulani, treat yourself to a stroll along the ocean on the paved walkway leading past the **Sheraton Waikiki** (2255 Kalakaua Ave.) to the gracious old **Royal Hawaiian Hotel** (2259 Kalakaua Ave.). The lovely lobby, with its pink decor, is reminiscent of another era. A stroll through the old gardens, with their tall swaying coconut palms and vivid flowers, is like stepping through a time warp to a period when Waikiki was a sleepy, tropical paradise with a couple of gracious old hotels.

The illusion is only momentary, for the path leads to the modern **Royal Hawaiian Shopping Center** (2201 Kalakaua Ave.). There are so many interesting shops tucked away here, it's a wonder that some of them are surviving, especially those on the upper floors (*see* Chapter 5).

Time Out A good treat to try while at the Royal Hawaiian mall is the local favorite, shave ice, the Hawaiian version of a snow cone, which comes in exotic fruit flavors like *lychee* and *li hing mui*. Have it with ice cream and *azuki* beans at the Island Snow stand.

Across the street from the Royal Hawaiian Shopping Center is the **Waikiki Business Plaza** (2270 Kalakaua Ave.), recognizable by its fish mosaic mural and little fountain. The **Hawaii Visitors Bureau** (tel. 808/923–1811) is on the eighth floor. Pick up free booklets on hotels, buses, and restaurants, as well as a calendar of events. On the 10th floor are some wholesale fashion outlets open to the public. This is a good place to end a day's walking tour, or to take a break before moving on.

Tour 2

Begin this tour at the Waikiki Business Plaza. Walking toward Diamond Head, in the middle of the same block, you can't miss the **International Market Place** (2330 Kalakaua Ave.) with its spreading banyan and Swiss Family Robinson–style treehouse. There's usually a lot of activity here, with woodcarvers, basket weavers, and other artisans from various Pacific islands creating and selling their handicrafts. Most of the souvenir stuff, both tacky and 24 karat, is sold from little Asian-style pushcarts.

Time Out The **Food Court** in the **Market Place** is a collection of individual food concessions with a central outdoor seating area. It includes inexpensive Japanese, Chinese, Korean, Filipino, Greek, Italian, and American kitchens.

If you can stand another shopping mall, turn mauka (toward mountains, north) on Kaiulani Avenue to **King's Village** (131 Kaiulani Ave.). It's ultra-cute, with cobblestone streets and salespeople in period garb. There's a Burger King here, and you can sit outside under umbrellas. A Changing of the Guard ceremony is enacted every evening at 6:15, with "soldiers" in monarchy-era uniforms.

If you take a short walk from King's Village in the direction of Diamond Head, you'll reach the **Hyatt Regency Waikiki** (2424

Kalakaua Ave.). To help visitors become acquainted with Hawaiian arts and crafts, Auntie Malia Solomon, resident Hawaiian authority for the Hyatt Regency, has assembled what she calls her "sharing place." The hotel calls the small second-floor museum of artifacts, quilts, and crafts **Hyatt's Hawaii.** It's a charming collection.

Time Out If you need to rest your feet, stop off at **Harry's Cafe and Bar,** which is right in the Hyatt Regency's atrium with a waterfall (on the ground floor). Harry's is a fun place to people-watch, and the inexpensive menu includes tasty sandwiches, homemade croissants, and other deli treats.

Across the way, the oldest hotel in Waikiki, the venerable **Moana,** has undergone a major historical renovation. Wander through the breezy lobby out to the wide back porch that looks out on the beach. They've done a beautiful job on this historic building. The Moana is now merged with the neighboring Surfrider Hotel and is renamed the **Sheraton Moana Surfrider** (2365 Kalakaua Ave.). There are period furnishings, historical exhibits, and plenty of nostalgia. The Beaux Arts–style hotel has been placed on the National Register of Historic Places. Visit the **Historical Room** in the Rotunda just above the main entrance, and enjoy a collection of old photographs and memorabilia dating from the opening of the hotel in 1901.

Next to the Sheraton Moana Surfrider are the four **Kahuna** (or **Wizard) Stones of Waikiki,** which, according to legend, were placed there in tribute to four prophets from Tahiti, who came to Hawaii sometime before the 16th century. Before disappearing, the prophets are said to have transferred their healing powers to the stones. They're by the beach showers, and, more often than not, are irreverently draped in wet towels.

Two blocks away at 2490 Kalakaua Avenue, with an entrance on Liliuokalani Avenue, is the **Pacific Beach Hotel,** with its huge 280,000-gallon aquarium. The aquarium is two stories high and harbors a thousand fish. The **Oceanarium Restaurant** is on the lobby level, and the hotel's fine dining room, **Neptune's,** is directly above it. Both wrap around the aquarium. *Tel. 808/922–1233. Admission free. Daily feeding times are 9 and 11:30 AM; 12:30, 5:30, 6:30, and 7:30 PM.*

If you walk two blocks toward Diamond Head, you'll find the only church in Waikiki with its own building, the Roman Catholic **Saint Augustine's** (130 Ohua Ave., tel. 808/923–7024).

Just around the corner, in back of the church, is the **Damien Museum,** a small but fascinating two-room exhibit centering on the life and work of the Belgian priest Father Joseph Damien de Veuster, who came to Hawaii and labored and died among the victims of Hansen's disease (leprosy) on the island of Molokai. Ask to see the museum's 20-minute videotape. It is low-budget, but well done and emotionally gripping. *Tel. 808/923–2690. Admission free. Open weekdays, 9–3, Sat. 9–noon.*

With much to think about, this is another good place to end a tour of Waikiki. The area in and around Kapiolani Park, next on the list, is worth a day's outing by itself to allow plenty of time to smell the flowers—and the fresh clean surf.

Tour 3

㉠ Start this tour at the **Honolulu Zoo** (151 Kapahulu Ave., on the corner of Kalakaua Ave. and Kapahulu Ave.), which is just a two-block walk toward Diamond Head from the Damien Museum. The zoo is 40 green acres of lush foliage and home to 2,000 furry and finned creatures. There are bigger and better zoos, but this one is pretty, and where else can you see a *nene*, Hawaii's state bird? On Wednesday evenings in the summer, the zoo offers "The Wildest Show in Town," a free program of singing, dancing, and other entertainment. Check the local newspaper, either the *Honolulu Advertiser* or *Star Bulletin*, for what's playing. Pack a picnic supper and join local families for a night out at the zoo. There is a new petting zoo and elephant show. *Tel. 808/971-7171. Admission: $1, children free. Open daily 8:30-4.*

Wednesdays, Saturdays, and Sundays, look for the **Zoo Fence Art Mart,** on Monsarrat Avenue outside the zoo, on the Diamond Head side. There's some affordable work by good contemporary artists that will make better souvenirs of Hawaii than some of the junky ashtrays and monkeypod Hawaiian gods carved in the Philippines.

㉑ ㉒ Across Monsarrat Avenue between Kalakaua Avenue and Paki Street, in **Kapiolani Park,** is the **Waikiki Shell,** Honolulu's outdoor concert arena. Check the newspaper to see what's playing. Local people bring a picnic and get "grass" seats (lawn seating). Here's a chance to have a magical night listening to some of the world's best musicians while lying on a blanket with the moon shining over Diamond Head.

㉓ In bleachers adjacent to the Waikiki Shell, the famous **Kodak Hula Show** has been wowing crowds for more than 50 years. It's colorful, lively, and fun. For the best seats, get there by 9:30 AM for the 10 AM one-hour show. Naturally, it's a great opportunity to take photographs. *Tel. 808/833-1661. Admission: $2.50. Shows Tues.-Thurs. only.*

㉔ Kapiolani Park's other major entertainment area is the **Kapiolani Bandstand.** There's usually a free show of some kind on Sunday afternoons at 2, frequently a concert by the Royal Hawaiian Band. Check the newspaper for particulars. Some excellent hula dances are performed here by local groups that don't frequent the hotels.

㉕ To save steps, cut diagonally across the park to the **Waikiki Aquarium** (2777 Kalakaua Ave.). Recently renovated, the amazing little aquarium harbors more than 300 species of Hawaiian and South Pacific marine life, including the giant clam, the chambered nautilus, and scary sharks. It's the third oldest aquarium in the United States. *Tel. 808/923-9741. Admission: $2.50, children under 15 free. Open daily 9-5.*

㉖ A little farther along Kalakaua Avenue toward Diamond Head is the **Waikiki War Memorial Natatorium.** This open-air structure was built to commemorate lives lost in World War II. Although the pool is not recommended for swimming (the eels have made it their home), the beach adjacent to the Natatorium offers some of the best swimming in Waikiki. The memorial, though showing wear and tear, stands proudly and was recently saved from a wrecker's ball. *Admission free. Open 9:30-5.*

Time Out Close by, at the **New Otani Kaimana Beach Hotel** (2863
Kalakaua Ave.), you can dine outdoors beside the sand in the
shade of a *hau* tree. This spot is not well known to tourists, but
it's one of the nicest oceanfront dining options on the island.

You might be lucky enough to spot *Magnum, P.I.* star Tom
Selleck on the sands in front of the **Outrigger Canoe Club,** one of
his favorite haunts. The club is private, but not the beach.

㉗ You could walk over to the **Kapiolani Park Rose Garden** at Paki
Street and Monsarrat Avenue, but it's a long walk, and if you
come from an area where roses thrive, you've probably seen
better. There are picnic tables and the admission is free.

A Waikiki Hike

For those willing to do more strenuous walking, the hike to the
㉘ summit of **Diamond Head** offers a marvelous view. Drive along
Diamond Head Road, on the Waikiki side of the extinct volcano.
The entrance to the crater is marked by a road sign. Drive
through the tunnel to the inside of the crater, once a military
fortification.

You can also take a bus from Waikiki. Bus No. 58, "Hawaii Kai-
Sea Life Park," stops near the entrance. A sign points the way.

The trail begins at the parking lot. Signs tell you that the hike
takes an hour, but you can probably do it in 40 minutes or less,
even with a child in tow. Most guidebooks also say there are 99
steps on the trail to the top. That's true of one flight, but there
are four flights altogether. Bring a flashlight to see your way
through a narrow tunnel. The view is worth it when you get
there, sweeping across Waikiki and Honolulu in one direction
and out to Koko Head in the other, with Diamond Head Lighthouse and surfers and windsurfers scattered like confetti on
the cresting waves below. *Park hours daily 6 AM–6 PM.*

You can also walk the 2.3 miles from the zoo to the crater and
then climb the additional .7 mile to the 760-foot summit. A
group meets Saturdays at 9 AM by the rainbow windsock at the
zoo entrance. All but the last part of the hike is escorted and
narrated by volunteer guides. Everyone gets a free souvenir "I
Climbed Diamond Head" badge. *Tel. 808/944–0804. Donation:
$3, free for children.*

A Waikiki Dive

An authentic submarine now operates just off Waikiki. *Atlantis,* which has been taking tourists down to the sea in ships at
Caribbean sites for many years, now does Waikiki dives aboard
a 65-foot, 80-ton sub carrying up to 46 passengers. Price includes a catamaran ride aboard the *Hilton Rainbow I* to the
dive site and a tour of the Waikiki and Diamond Head shoreline.
The sub dives up to 100 feet to see a sunken Navy yard oiler and
an artificial reef populated by brilliant fish. While the man-
made concrete reef looks more like a fish tenement, it is drawing reef fish back to the area. *Hilton Port, Hilton Hawaiian
Village Hotel, tel. 808/522–1710. $67 adults, $33.50 children 4–
12. Note: Flash photography will not work. Use film speed 200
or above without flash.*

Waikiki Beaches

The 2½-mile strand called Waikiki Beach is actually a lei of beaches extending from the Hilton Hawaiian Village on one end to Diamond Head on the other. All of Hawaii's beaches are public, so you can plunk down with aplomb in front of the most elegant hotel.

There are some words of caution to keep in mind when approaching any Hawaiian beach. Take notice of the signs. If they warn of dangerous surf conditions or currents, pay attention. Before you stretch out beneath a swaying palm, check it for coconuts. The trade winds can bring them tumbling down on top of you with enough force to cause serious injury. And don't forget the sunscreen. The sun-protection factor in some new preparations now goes higher than 29. It's a good idea to reapply sunscreen after swimming. Waikiki is only 21 degrees north of the equator, and the ultraviolet rays are much more potent than they are at home. Also, no alcoholic beverages are allowed on the beaches, which is why you may notice some people drinking out of brown paper bags.

Kahanamoku Beach and Lagoon. The swimming is good here, the surf is gentle, and the snorkeling is not bad. You may find the water in the lagoon a touch too torpid, but it's perfect for small children, and you can lazily paddle around in a little boat. The area is named for Hawaii's famous Olympic swimming champion, Duke Kahanamoku. There's a snack concession, a surfboard and beach-equipment rental shop, showers, catamaran cruises, and a sand volleyball court. *Fronting the Hilton Hawaiian Village.*

Fort DeRussy Beach. This is the widest part of Waikiki Beach, and it trails off to a coral ocean bottom. There are volleyball courts, food stands, picnic tables, dressing rooms and showers, and snack concessions. The beach is frequented by military personnel but is open to everyone. *Fronting Fort DeRussy and the Hale Koa Hotel.*

Gray's Beach. A little lodging house called Gray's-by-the-Sea once stood on this site, and it left its name behind. The Hawaiians used to consider this a place for spiritual healing and baptism and called it *Kawehewehe* (the removal). High tides often cover the narrow beach here. Beyond the reef are two good surfing spots, called Paradise and Number Threes. You'll also find food concessions, surfboard and beach-equipment rental shops, and canoe and catamaran rides. *Fronting the Halekulani Hotel.*

Kahaloa and Ulukou Beaches. Probably the best swimming, and certainly the most activity, is at this little stretch of Waikiki Beach. There are snack bars, catamaran rides, and outrigger-canoe rides, and you can sign up for a surfing lesson. The Royal Hawaiian Hotel cordons off a small section of sand for its guests, bringing to mind a rich kid's sandbox. The heart of beach activities is the Waikiki Beach Center. Facilities include public rest rooms, changing rooms, showers, and a snack stand. The police station is located here. *Fronting the Royal Hawaiian Hotel and Sheraton Moana Surfrider.*

Kuhio Beach Park. A seawall jutting into the ocean acts as a breakwater to keep shoreside waters calm. The area is deceptive, though, and children should be watched closely, because there are unpredictable deep holes in spots. (There have been several drownings here.) Beyond the wall, surfers and bodysurfers ride the waves. The wall is a great place for sunset watching, but be careful of your footing. *Extending from the Waikiki Beach Center to the wall.*

Queen's Surf. Beyond the seawall, toward Diamond Head, is what is known as the other end of Waikiki, where beaches beginning with Queen's Surf Beach—named for Queen Liliuokalani's beach house which once stood here—laze along the makai (south) side of Kapiolani Park. The sand is softer than by the hotels, and the beach slopes gently to the water. A mixture of families and gays gathers here, and it seems as if someone always has a bongo drum. There's a lawn, good shade trees, picnic tables, and a changing house with showers. This is a nice place for a sunset picnic. *Across from the entrance to the Honolulu Zoo.*

Sans Souci. This small rectangle of sand, a favorite with singles, is nicknamed Dig-Me Beach due to its outlandish display of skimpy bathing suits. The waters it borders are shallow and safe for children, and the spot draws many ocean kayakers and outrigger canoers. Serious swimmers and triathletes also swim in the channel here, beyond the reef. The beach also features a pair of outdoor showers (no changing house) and a grassy area that is popular with picnickers and volleyball buffs. The beach wall is a good vantage point for sunset watching. There's no food concession, but adjacent to one end of the beach is the Hau Tree Lanai, a wonderful open-air eatery that is part of the hotel. *Makai side of Kapiolani Park, between the New Otani Kaimana Beach Hotel and the Waikiki War Memorial Natatorium.*

Waikiki for Free

Aside from the obvious things like sunshine and sand, there are many attractions and events in Waikiki and around the island of Oahu that are free.

This section includes both attractions that are covered elsewhere in the book and additional attractions that are described here for the first time. They are divided into those that are in Waikiki and those that are beyond Waikiki, and they are listed alphabetically. Also, many hotels provide free hula lessons, lei-making classes, exercise sessions, and other entertainment for their guests. Be sure to check your hotel's activities desk.

In Waikiki **Chinese cooking class.** Learn to prepare classic Chinese dishes and sample the results at the Great Wok of China restaurant. *Royal Hawaiian Shopping Center, 2233 Kalakaua Ave., Bldg. B, 3rd floor, tel. 808/922–5373. Fri. 11:30 AM.*

Damien Museum (*see* Tour 2 in Exploring Waikiki, above).

Exercise class. Bring a towel or mat for an outdoor session on the lawn. *Fort De Russy Beach, in front of the Hale Koa Hotel, 2055 Kalia Rd., Mon.–Sat 9 AM; closed Sun.*

Fashion show. The latest resort fashions are paraded through the beautiful atrium of the Hyatt Regency Waikiki by Hawaii's top models. *2424 Kalakaua Ave., tel. 808/923–1234. Wed. 4 PM.*

Honolulu marathon clinic. Lectures and instructions on running are given by experts, then participants break into groups, depending on level of ability and experience, for a run around the park. *Kapiolani Bandstand, Kapiolani Park, tel. 808/734–7200. Sun. 7:30 AM.*

Hula lessons. Learn the real hula from a certified hula teacher. *Royal Hawaiian Shopping Center, 2201 Kalakaua Ave., Bldg. C, 3rd floor, tel. 808/922–0588. Mon., Wed., and Fri. 10:30 AM.*

Karate. Take a lesson in one of the Asian martial arts. *Waikiki Community Center, 310 Paokalani Ave., tel. 808/923–1802. T'ai chi lessons (another martial art) are given Wed. and Fri. 11 AM.*

King's Village (*see* Tour 2 in Exploring Waikiki, above).

Polynesian Cultural Center Mini Show. The enthusiastic young entertainers from Hawaii's number-one paid visitor attraction stage a miniproduction. Of course they're hoping you'll rush right into their Waikiki ticket office and sign up for the complete package, but there's no pressure. *Royal Hawaiian Shopping Center, 2201 Kalakaua Ave., Bldg. C, 1st floor, tel. 808/922–0588. Tues., Thurs., Sat. 9:30 AM.*

Porpoise Feeding. Kahala Hilton (*see* What to See and Do with Children, below).

Tennis courts. For public courts in Waikiki, *see* Participant Sports in Chapter 6.

Wildest Show in Town. The zoo, which normally charges admission, is free after 4 PM. A free show is staged under the big banyan tree. The bill includes a wide variety of entertainment from rock to puppet shows. *Honolulu Zoo, 151 Kapahulu Ave., tel. 808/971–7171. June, July, and Aug. only, Wed. 6PM.*

Evening at City Hall. A free concert is offered on the fourth Thursday of each month in the courtyard of City Hall. *King and Punchbowl Sts., tel. 808/527–5666. Concerts start at 7 PM.*

Zoo Fence Art Mart (*see* Tour 3 in Exploring Waikiki, above).

Beyond Waikiki *Arizona* **Memorial** (*see* Tour 4 in Chapter 4).

East-West Center. Located on the University of Hawaii campus, the center was founded to promote understanding among the people of Asia, the Pacific, and the United States. There are some fascinating buildings and gardens, especially the Japanese garden. The center offers free tours. Reservations are not required, except for groups. Meet at Jefferson Hall. *1777 East-West Rd., tel. 808/944–7691. Bus No. 4 "Nuuanu-Dowsett" from Waikiki. Wed. 1:30 PM.*

Humanities Conversation. A lecture and discussion on history, literature, philosophy, or culture is held by the Hawaii Committee for the Humanities. *1802 Keeaumoku St., Honolulu, tel. 808/732–5402. First Wed. of each month, 4 PM. No meetings in January. Shuttle bus No. 17 from Ala Moana Shopping Center.*

Hawaii State Capitol. The architecture of this building, which is surrounded by a moat and held up by volcano-shaped columns, was inspired by Hawaii's unique island geography and geology and by the prevailing spirit of aloha. Legislative sessions are open to the public. Take a free one-hour tour, which includes a visit to the offices of Governor John Waihee and Lieutenant Governor Ben Cayetano. Arrange a tour by stopping in at the Sargeant-at-Arms office, Room 036. You should probably make reservations to ensure that there will be a guide available. *415 S. Beretania St., tel. 808/548–7851. Weekdays 8–5. Bus No. 2 from Waikiki.*

Helemano Plantation. Five acres of flowers, fruits, and vegetables are maintained by disabled citizens working in a vocational training program. It also offers classes in lei making and hula. A gift shop and restaurant are on the site. *64-1510 Kamehameha Hwy., adjacent to the Dole Pineapple Pavilion, tel. 808/622–3929. Daily 7:30–5. Bus No. 8, 19, or 20 from Waikiki to Ala Moana Shopping Center, then transfer to No. 55, "Circle Island," going west.*

Honolulu Hale. The lovely Spanish Colonial-style building is Honolulu's city hall. There are often art exhibits showing the work of local artists. At Christmas, the lobby is filled with decorated trees and becomes one of Honolulu's prime attractions. A free booklet describing the building is available from the mayor's office on the third floor. *Corner of King and Punchbowl Sts., tel. 808/523–4385. Bus No. 2 from Waikiki.*

Hoomaluhia Botanic Garden Guided Nature Walk. Exotic flora from around the world are growing in this 400-acre garden. Bring light rain gear, insect repellent, and lunch. Reservations are necessary. *End of Luluku Rd., Kaneohe, tel. 808/235–6636. Sat. 10 AM for a 3.4-mi walk; Sun. 12:30 PM for a 2-mi walk. Bus No. 55 "Kaneohe" from Ala Moana Shopping Center.*

Iolani Palace grounds. The Royal Hawaiian Band holds a free concert every Friday from 12:15 to 1. Pick up a picnic lunch, sit on the lawn, and enjoy the music. This series is popular with the downtown office workers. *King and Richards Sts., tel. 808/527–5666.*

Kaneaki Heiau. An impressive ancient Hawaiian temple has been partially restored and includes a prayer tower and several thatched buildings on massive stone platforms. It is located beyond the Sheraton Makaha Resort. *Phone Sheraton's guest services desk, tel. 808/695–9511, to be sure it's open before the long ride out. 84-626 Makaha Valley Rd. Tues.–Sun. 10–2; closed Mon. Bus No. 51 "Makaha" from Ala Moana Shopping Center.*

Kawaiahao Church (*see* Tour 1 in Chapter 4).

Keaiwa Heiau State Park. This temple of the old religion of Hawaii was used as a place of healing. Labeled medicinal plants are maintained by the state parks division. The park also contains the Aiea Loop Trail, an easy 4.8-mile mountain hike. Look for the remains of a Japanese plane that crashed into the mountain during the attack on Pearl Harbor. *Aiea Heights Dr., tel. 808/548–3179. Open 7–4. Bus No. 11 "Aiea Heights" from Ala Moana Shopping Center.*

Koko Head Shoreline (*see* Tour 3 in Chapter 4).

Lyon Arboretum. Affiliated with the University of Hawaii, this 200-acre garden is tucked in lush Manoa valley, adjacent to the popular (and paying) tourist attraction, Paradise Park. It features a wide variety of tropical flora. *3860 Manoa Rd., tel. 808/988–3177. Open weekdays 9–3, Sat. 9–12; closed Sun. Free* *guided tours first Fri. and third Wed. at 1 PM, third Sat. at 10 AM. Bus No. 5 from Ala Moana Shopping Center to the end of the line, a 45-min ride.*

Mayor's Aloha Friday Music Break. Downtown office workers gather around the fountains at lunch to enjoy a concert. The entertainment is varied and may be anything from a school choir to one of the big-name Hawaii groups. There are several fastfood restaurants bordering the square, so you can pick up a picnic. *Tamarind Park, corner of Bishop and King Sts., tel. 808/527–5666. Fri. only, noon. Bus No. 2 from Waikiki.*

Royal Mausoleum. Six of Hawaii's eight monarchs are buried in this 3-acre plot: Kings Kamehameha II, III, IV, V, Kalakaua, and Queen Liliuokalani. *2261 Nuuanu Ave., Honolulu. Weekdays 8–4. Bus No. 4 "Nuuanu" from Waikiki.*

Tennent Art Foundation Gallery. The works of celebrated Island artist Madge Tennent are displayed here. Her subjects are Polynesian and her interpretations are massive in stature, conveying both power and a sensuous softness. *203 Prospect St., tel. 808/531–1987. Tues.–Sat. 10–2; Sun. 2–4. Bus No. 15 from the main depot.*

Young People's Hula Show. The Kapiolani Butterworth children's hula group presents the songs and dances of various Pacific islands. The young dance students are delightful. *Ala Moana Shopping Center, Ala Moana Blvd. and Atkinson Dr., tel. 808/946–2811. Sun. 9:30 AM. Bus No. 8, 19, or 20 from Waikiki.*

What to See and Do with Children

A full moon over Diamond Head, the sound of the surf, the romantic strumming of a ukulele, flower-perfumed air, a gentle breeze—and the kids? Friends may think you've gone over to the far side, but in Waikiki it is possible to have it all—romance and good family fun. Hawaii is a family-centered society, and Waikiki, surprisingly, is a family kind of place. When you need time on your own, many hotels have excellent baby-sitting services and exciting summer and holiday programs to keep your children entertained.

The Hawaiian word for child is *keiki* (CAKE-ee). Many restaurants offer special keiki menus. There are keiki events and keiki admissions to attractions at reduced rates or for free.

The beach is the big draw. With a shallow, sandy bottom, reef-protected waters, and gentle waves, **Waikiki Beach** is safe. There are concessions all along the strand for snacks, and umbrella and raft rental (*see* Waikiki Beaches, above). You can sign up the children for surfing lessons to learn Hawaii's sport of kings. Catamaran sails take the family to sea for an hour, a half-day snorkel trip, or a sunset cruise. There are outrigger canoe rides and aqua-bikes (*see* Participant Sports in Chapter 6). The best swimming spots for children are the walled-in area in front of the Holiday Inn and the lagoon at the Hilton Hawaiian Village. There are playground fixtures at **Queen's Surf Beach.** All beaches in Hawaii are open to the public. Be sure to use sunscreen on young skin, and reapply often.

Other Waikiki attractions especially for children include:

Honolulu Zoo. There's a petting zoo, an elephant show, a Farm in the Zoo and a tower to climb to look the giraffes right in the eye (*see* Tour 3 in Exploring Waikiki, above).

Zoo Fence Art Mart. On Wednesdays, Saturdays, and Sundays there's usually an artist who will do while-you-wait pastel portraits of children.

Waikiki Aquarium. *2777 Kalakaua Ave. Tel. 808/923–9741. Admission: $2.50 adults over 16. Open daily 9–5.*

Kapiolani Park. Adjacent to the zoo, it offers 140 acres in which to run free. There's good family fun at the Kodak Hula Show, including children's hula lessons (*see* Tour 3 in Exploring Waikiki, above). *Admission: $2.50 adults.*

Diamond Head Hike. It takes a 6-year-old hiker 40 minutes to get to the top. Bring a flashlight for the tunnel.

U.S. Army Museum at Fort DeRussy. This is for young Rambo fans. (*see* Tour 1 in Exploring Waikiki, above).

Pacific Beach Hotel. One thousand fish live in the lobby of this hotel, housed in a 280,000-gallon aquarium (*see* Tour 2 in Exploring Waikiki, above).

Kahala Hilton Hotel. A lagoon with porpoises is the feature. *5000 Kahala Ave., tel. 808/734–2211. Feeding times: 11 AM; 2, and 4.*

Hilton Hawaiian Village Hotel. The newly landscaped grounds are practically a bird park with macaws, flamingoes, penguins, and more. *2005 Kalia Rd., tel. 808/949–4321.*

Ilikai Waikiki Hotel. A glass elevator whisks you to its top-floor Annabelle's lounge with breathtaking views. Try a frosty virgin chichi for the children. It's coconut and pineapple juice minus the alcohol. The elevator operates from 5 PM. *1777 Ala Moana Blvd., tel. 808/949–3811.*

Beyond Waikiki   **Hawaii Children's Museum.** The theme of the museum is "You the Child," with opportunities to learn about the body, tracing a family tree, and ethnic heritage, plus a Bug Zoo. *Dole Cannery Sq., 650 Iwilei Rd., Honolulu 96817, tel. 808/522–0040. Admission: $5 adults, $3 children 3–8. Closed Mon.*

Hawaii Maritime Center. Many of the center's exhibits are targeted for children. Climb aboard a reproduction of a Matson liner, see a whaling film, explore a real four-masted sailing ship.

Paradise Park. Visitors enter through a huge aviary. The highlight is the performing bird show, 10:25 AM and 1:30 and 3:30 PM. Other attractions: nature walks, "Animal Quackers Review," "Dancing Waters" lighted fountain show, having your picture taken with magnificent macaws.

Polynesian Cultural Center. You get around this 40-acre park by tram, canoe, or on foot. Children will have so much fun they won't even notice they're getting an education (*see* Tour 4 in Chapter 4).

Sea Life Park (*see* Tour 3 in Chapter 4).

Waimea Falls Park. Bring along swimsuits for the children—they'll enjoy a dunk under the falls (*see* Tour 4 in Chapter 4).

Restaurants Hawaii has most of the big burger and fried-chicken chains. There are also some unique restaurants offering more than food. The restaurants outlined here are not necessarily recommended for their food, but for some feature that children will enjoy. In all cases, the meals are acceptable.

Oceanarium. The restaurant wraps around the huge aquarium and its feeding times are scheduled at the diners' mealtimes. *Pacific Beach Hotel, 2490 Kalakaua Ave., tel. 808/922–1233. Reservations recommended. Dress: casual. AE, DC, MC, V. Inexpensive.*

Bobby McGee's Conglomeration. The staff dress in costume: Robin Hood may present the menu and bring the steaks. *2885 Kalakaua Ave., tel. 808/922–1282. Reservations recommended. Dress: aloha. AE, DC, MC, V. Dinner only, Mon.–Thurs. 5:30–10, Fri. and Sat. 5–11, Sun. 5–10. Moderate.*

The Willows. Keikis will like the ponds of prize carp and the thatched-roof pavilions. Famous "sky high" pies for dessert, in flavors like banana or macadamia nut, make this a favorite of small diners (*see* Chapter 7).

Pagoda. Japanese and American cuisine is served in a setting of Japanese gardens and carp ponds. The carp are fed daily at 8 AM, noon, and 6 PM. *Near Waikiki at 1525 Rycroft St., tel. 808/941–6611. Reservations recommended. Dress: aloha. AE, DC, MC, V. Daily lunch and dinner. Moderate.*

Hard Rock Cafe. Mom and Dad might appreciate the music history, and the little ones will go for the loud tunes, surf boards on the walls, and the Cadillac suspended over the bar. The burgers are great. *1826 Kalakaua Ave., tel. 808/955–7383. Reservations unnecessary. Dress: aloha. AE, DC, MC, V. Daily lunch and dinner. Moderate.*

Makai Market. Located in the Ala Moana Shopping Center, the market offers 20 separate food outlets and one central seating area. The children can have their fries and pizza while you dine on Thai, Japanese, Chinese, or health food, all at bargain prices (*see* Chapter 5).

Food Court. International Market Place. Separate food outlets and one central seating area offer Greek, Japanese, Chinese, Korean, Filipino, and burger and rib fare. *Inexpensive (see* Tour 2 in Exploring Waikiki, above).

Island Treats **Shave ice.** A local version of the snow cone. Order it with ice cream but skip the azuki beans—children will hate the beans.

Manapua. A rice-flour bun with Chinese-style meat filling is the local equivalent of a hamburger.

Crack Seed. This is a popular treat with Island children. It is an acquired taste. A good flavor for beginners is wet mango.

4 Excursions from Waikiki

Tour 1: Historic Downtown Honolulu

Numbers in the margin correspond with points of interest on the Downtown Honolulu map.

Honolulu's past and present play a delightful counterpoint throughout the downtown sector. Modern skyscrapers stand directly across the street from a series of piers where huge ocean liners come to call, as they have for decades. To reach this area from Waikiki by car, take Ala Moana Boulevard to Alakea Street. Turn right, and drive mauka (toward the mountains) three blocks to Hotel Street. Turn right, and right again on Richards Street, where there is a municipal parking lot. You can also try the metered parking in the Aloha Tower parking lot, across Ala Moana Boulevard from Alakea Street.

If you travel by public transportation, take the No. 2 bus from Waikiki. Get off at Alapai Street and walk makai (toward the ocean) to King Street. Most of the historic sites are clustered within easy walking distance.

❶ Begin this tour at the **Hawaii Maritime Center,** which is across Ala Moana Boulevard from Alakea Street in downtown Honolulu. Opened in late 1988, it features such attractions as the *Falls of Clyde*, a century-old, four-masted, square-rigged ship now used as a museum. Pier 7 was the international steamship pier in turn-of-the-century Honolulu. Aloha Tower, built in 1926 and once the tallest building in Hawaii, provides a panoramic view of the city and coastline. The Kalakaua Boat House includes exhibits covering Hawaii's whaling days, the history of Honolulu Harbor, and canoes, plus the Pacific Ocean Theater and open-air restaurants. *The Hokule'a* is a double-hulled canoe used on the Polynesian Voyaging Society's "Voyage of Rediscovery" to the South Pacific. *Pier 7, Ala Moana Blvd., Honolulu, tel. 808/536–6373. Admission: $6. Open daily 9–5.*

The **Children's Touch and Feel Museum** is also part of the Hawaii Maritime Center. At this 1,000-square-foot aquatic attraction, kids can play captain of a mock submarine complete with periscope, engine, steering and diving controls, and crew's quarters. A lifeboat and the deck of a 19th-century sailing vessel with steering wheel, capstan, and cargo winch, are also here to explore. A cassette tour narrated by William Conrad guides you through the museum. *Pier 7, Ala Moana Blvd., Honolulu, tel. 808/536–6373. Admission: $6 adults, $3 ages 6–17. Open 9–5.*

❷ Cross Ala Moana Boulevard, walk a block ewa (away from Diamond Head) and turn mauka (toward the mountains) on **Fort Street Mall,** a pedestrian walkway that passes buildings historic and new. Sit on a bench for a few minutes and watch the fascinating parade of everyone from businesspeople to street preachers.

❸ Turn left on King Street, and in a few blocks you'll reach **Chinatown,** the old section of downtown Honolulu, which is crammed with interesting shops. Slightly on the tawdry side, it has lately been getting a piecemeal face-lift as little art galleries open up in renovated structures. There are lei stands, herb shops, acupuncture studios, noodle factories, Chinese and Thai restaurants, and the colorful Oahu Market, an open-air emporium with hanging pig heads, display cases of fresh fish, row af-

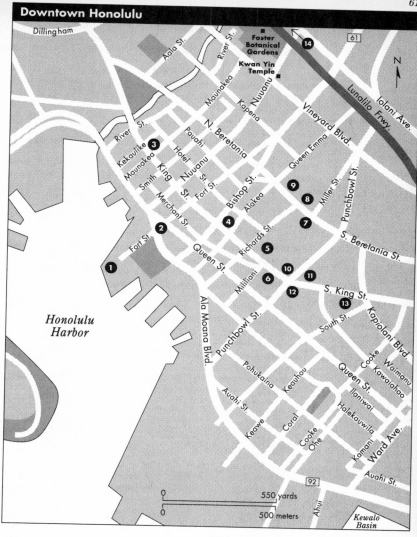

Aliiolani Hale
(Kamehameha I
statue), **6**

Bishop Museum, **14**

Chinatown, **3**

Fort Street Mall, **2**

Hawaii Maritime
Center, **1**

Hawaii State
Capitol, **7**

Hawaii State
Library, **10**

Honolulu Hale, **11**

Iolani Palace, **5**

Kawaiahao Church, **12**

Mission Houses
Museum, **13**

Saint Andrew's
Cathedral, **9**

Tamarind Park, **4**

Washington Place, **8**

ter row of exotic fruits and vegetables, and plenty of smiling vendors of all ethnic backgrounds.

Time Out There are plenty of fun Chinese restaurants in Chinatown, but **Wo Fat** (115 N. Hotel St., one block north of King St., tel. 808/ 537–6260) is a great lunchtime stop on your walking tour. Reputed to be Hawaii's oldest restaurant, this Hotel Street landmark has been doing business since 1882, with no indication of slowing down. Authentic Cantonese food is the fare in this three-story establishment with tile floors, and the meals are a great bargain. Be sure to order some of Wo Fat's special fried noodles with beef in oyster sauce.

❹ Walk back toward Diamond Head along King Street until it intersects with Bishop Street. On the mauka (mountain) side is lovely **Tamarind Park,** where folks gather at lunchtime to hear live music, from jazz and Hawaiian to the U.S. Marine band. Check the newspaper to find out the schedule. Friday is the most likely day to catch an act. Do as the locals do: Pick up lunch at one of the many carryouts bordering the park, pull up a bench or some lawn, and enjoy. *Admission free. Open all day.*

❺ Continue along King Street until you reach **Iolani Palace,** on the mauka side. This graceful Victorian structure was built by King David Kalakaua on the site of an earlier palace. Beautifully restored, it is America's only royal palace and contains the thrones of King Kalakaua and his successor (and sister) Queen Liliuokalani. Also on the palace grounds is the **Kalakaua Coronation Bandstand,** where the Royal Hawaiian Band performs at noon most Fridays. Stop at the **Iolani Barracks,** built to house the Royal Guard and now a gift shop. *King St. at Richards St., tel. 808/522–0832. Reservations required. Admission: $4 adults, $1 children 5–12; children under 5 are not permitted. Open only for guided tours, Wed.–Sat. 9–2:15.*

❻ Across King Street from the palace is **Aliiolani Hale,** the old judiciary building that once served as the parliament hall during the monarchy era. In front of it is the gilded **statue of Kamehameha I,** the Big Island chieftain who united all the warring Hawaiian Islands into one kingdom. He stands with one arm outstretched in welcome. The original of this statue is on the Big Island, in Kapaau, near the birthplace of the king. Each year on June 11, his birthday, the Honolulu statue is draped in leis.

❼ Walk one block mauka up Richards Street to see the **Hawaii State Capitol** (S. Beretania St. between Punchbowl and Richards Sts., tel. 808/548–5420). Built in 1969, this architectural gem is richly symbolic: The columns look like palm trees, the legislative chambers are shaped like volcanic cinder cones, and the central court is open to the sky, representing Hawaii's open society. The capitol is surrounded by reflecting pools, just as the Islands are embraced by water. Between the capitol and the palace is a statue of Queen Liliuokalani, Hawaii's last reigning monarch. In front is a statue of Father Damien, the Belgian priest who gave his life caring for the victims of Hansen's disease, or leprosy, on the island of Molokai.

❽ Almost across the street from the state capitol is **Washington Place** (320 S. Beretania St.). This graceful 1846 mansion is currently the home of Hawaii's governor. Queen Liliuokalani lived here until her death in 1917. You can only peer through the wrought-iron gates, since the residence is not open to the public.

9 Next to Washington Place is **Saint Andrew's Cathedral** (S. Beretania St. at Queen Emma St.), Episcopal headquarters in Hawaii. Queen Emma, widow of Kamehameha IV, supervised the construction of the church and was baptized in the sanctuary. The building was designed in England, and parts of it were shipped from there.

Time Out   Walk back to King Street and continue one block farther, to Merchant Street. Turn right and you'll discover a charming open-air restaurant ideal for lunch, a snack, or a cool drink. True to its name, the **Croissanterie** (222 Merchant St., tel. 808/ 533–3443) features fresh-baked breads, muffins, and croissants, great for sandwiches or on their own. Order a beer or a cup of Hawaii's own Lion Coffee, get a salad with your sandwich, and enjoy the relaxed atmosphere of this homey indoor-outdoor spot. In the restaurant's basement, you'll find a used bookstore, complete with bargain volumes on Hawaii and the Pacific.

10 Return to King Street, stay on the mauka side, and proceed in a Diamond Head direction. Past the palace is the **Hawaii State Library**, whose "Asia and the Pacific" room has a fascinating collection of books old and new about Hawaii's history. The library was under renovation at press time, but should reopen in early 1992. *478 King St., tel. 808/548–4775. Open Tues. and Thurs. 9–8; Mon., Wed., Fri., and Sat. 9–5.*

11 Next on the mauka side is **Honolulu Hale,** or City Hall (530 S. King St. at Punchbowl St.), a Mediterranean/Renaissance-style building constructed in 1929. You can walk into the cool, open-ceiling lobby, which sometimes displays works by local artists.

12 Across the street, on the corner of King and Punchbowl, is **Kawaiahao Church,** Hawaii's most famous religious structure. Fancifully called Hawaii's Westminster Abbey, the coral-block church witnessed the coronations, weddings, and funerals of generations of Hawaiian royalty. The graves of missionaries and of King Lunalilo are in the yard. The upper gallery has an exhibit of paintings of the royal families. *957 Punchbowl St. at King St., tel. 808/522–1333. Services in English and Hawaiian each Sun. morning at 10:30. Free tours Mon.–Fri. 9–12 and Sun. after the service. Call ahead to schedule one.*

13 On the Diamond Head side of the church is the **Mission Houses Museum,** a historic complex where the first American missionaries in Hawaii lived. Arriving in 1820, the stalwart band gained royal favor and influenced every aspect of island life. Their descendants have become leaders in government and business. The white frame house was prefabricated in New England and shipped around the Horn. *553 S. King St., tel. 808/ 531–0481. Admission: $3.50 adults, $1 children 6–15. Museum can be seen only on a guided tour, which is held once an hour, with the last tour at 3. Open Tues.–Sat. 9–4, Sun. noon–4. Closed New Year's Day, Easter, Thanksgiving, and Christmas.*

Tour 2: A Side Trip to the Bishop Museum and Planetarium

Anyone who is interested in any facet of Hawaiian or Pacific culture should make the time to take this special tour. The building alone, with its huge Victorian turrets and immense stone walls, is a sight worth seeing.

Founded in 1889 by Charles R. Bishop as a memorial to his **14** wife, Princess Bernice Pauahi, the **Bishop Museum** began as a repository for the royal possessions of this last direct descendant of King Kamehameha the Great. It has since achieved world fame as a center of Polynesian archaeology, ethnology, and history.

There are lustrous feather capes, scary god images, the skeleton of a giant sperm whale, an authentic, well-preserved grass house, and changing displays of old photographs and ethnic crafts. The planetarium next door spotlights "Polynesian Skies," a narrated show that helps you unravel the mysteries of the tropical skies. Arts and crafts demonstrations take place regularly. *1525 Bernice St., tel. 808/848–4129. Admission: $5.95 adults, children under 6 free, including the planetarium. Open Mon.–Sat. 9–5 and the first Sun. of each month, which is "Family Sunday." Closed Christmas. By car, take Lunalilo Fwy. to Houghtailing exit. Make an immediate right on Houghtailing St., then a left onto Bernice St. By public transportation, take Bus No. 2 ("School Street") from Waikiki. Get off at the Kamehameha Shopping Center, walk makai (toward the ocean) 1 block to Bernice St., then go left.*

Tour 3: A Driving Tour of the East Oahu Ring

Numbers in the margin correspond with points of interest on the Oahu map.

From Waikiki, there are two routes to Lunalilo Freeway (H-1). On the Diamond Head end, go mauka (toward the mountains) on Kapahulu Avenue and follow the signs to the freeway. On the ewa (away from Diamond Head) end, take Ala Wai Boulevard and turn mauka at Kalakaua Avenue, staying on it until it ends at Beretania Street, which is one-way going left. Turn right off Beretania at Piikoi Street, and the signs will direct you onto the freeway heading west.

Take the freeway exit marked **Pali Highway,** one of two roads that cut through the Koolau Mountains.

1 On the right is the **Queen Emma Summer Palace.** The colonial-style white mansion, which once served as the summer retreat of King Kamehameha IV and his wife, Queen Emma, is now a museum maintained by the Daughters of Hawaii. It contains many excellent examples of koa furniture of the period, including the beautiful cradle of Prince Albert, heir to the throne, who died at age four. *2913 Pali Hwy., tel. 808/595–3167. Admission: $4. Guided tours daily 9–4. Closed Thanksgiving, Christmas, New Year's Eve, Easter, and July 4.*

As you drive toward the summit of the highway, the road is lined with sweet ginger during the summer and red poinsettias during the winter. If it has been raining, waterfalls will be tumbling down the sheer, chiseled cliffs of the Koolaus, creating a veritable wonderland in green.

② Watch for the turn to the **Pali Lookout** (Nuuanu Pali). There is a small parking lot and a lookout wall from which you can see all the way up and down the windward coast—a view that Mark Twain called the most beautiful in the world. It was in this region that King Kamehameha I drove defending forces over the edges of the 1,000-foot-high cliffs, thus winning the decisive battle for control of Oahu.

As you descend the highway on the other side of the mountain, continue straight along what becomes Kailua Road. If you are interested in Hawaiian history, look for the YMCA at the Castle Hospital junction of Kalanianaole Highway and Kailua
③ Road. Behind it is **Ulu Po Heiau.** Though it may look like a pile of rocks to the uninitiated, Ulu Po Heiau is a sacred platform for the worship of the gods that dates back to ancient times.

④ If you're ready for a detour to **Kailua Beach,** which many people consider the best on the island, continue straight on Kailua Beach Road, no matter how many times the road changes its name, until it forms a "T" with Kalaheo Avenue.

Make a right on Kalaheo and continue until you come to the corner of Kailua Road. On one side is the **Kalapawai Market.** Generations of children have gotten their beach snacks here, and you might like to as well, since there's no concession stand at Kailua Beach. Across the street is the **Kailua Beach Center,** where you can rent windsurfing equipment and arrange for lessons at **Kailua Sailboards** (tel. 808/262–2555; *see* Sports, below, for further information). **Naish Hawaii** (tel. 808/262–6068) and **Windsurfing Hawaii** (tel. 808/261–3539) also offer rental equipment in nearby Kailua. **Wild Bill's Sandwich Saloon** (tel. 808/261–5518) will fix you up with a great boxed lunch to take with you to the beach.

Past the market, the road crosses a little bridge. On your left is Kailua Beach Park, where there are showers and picnic areas, plus a small parking lot (*see* Beaches Around Oahu, below). On a windy day, you'll see scores of windsurfing enthusiasts rigging their sails on the grass. At the beach, everyone from beginners to international pro Robbie Naish can be seen boardsailing on the aqua waters of Kailua Bay.

Retracing your route back to Castle Junction, turn left at the intersection onto Kalanianaole Highway. Soon you will come to
⑤ the town of **Waimanalo,** traditionally a depressed area. Down the side roads, heading mauka, are little farms that grow a variety of fruits and flowers. Toward the back of the valley, flanked by cliffs, are small ranches with grazing horses. In a small shopping plaza on the makai (ocean) side of the road, there's a **Dave's Ice Cream** (41-1537 Kalanianaole Hwy., tel. 808/259–8576), which has some of the best ice cream in the Islands, including such exotic, tropical flavors as lychee and mango.

If you see any trucks selling corn on the cob and you're staying at a place where you can cook it, be sure to get some. It may be the sweetest you'll ever eat, and the price is the lowest on Oahu.

⑥ **Bellows Beach** (off Kalanianaole Hwy. in Bellows Air Force Station) is open weekends and holidays. The entrance is on the makai (ocean) side of the highway. The beach is uncrowded and great for swimming and bodysurfing. There's shade as well as picnic areas (*see* Beaches Around Oahu, below).

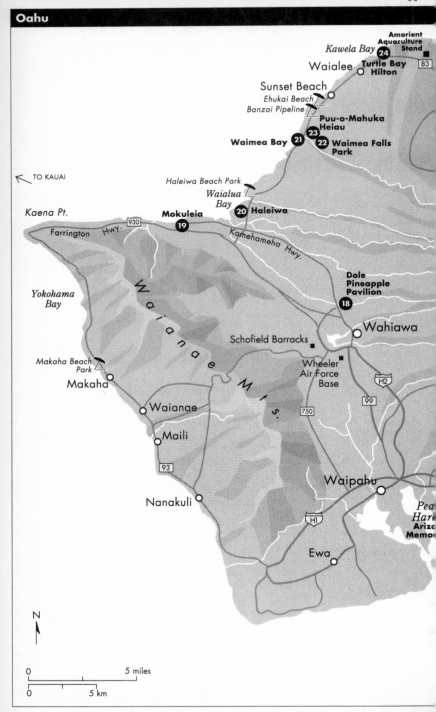

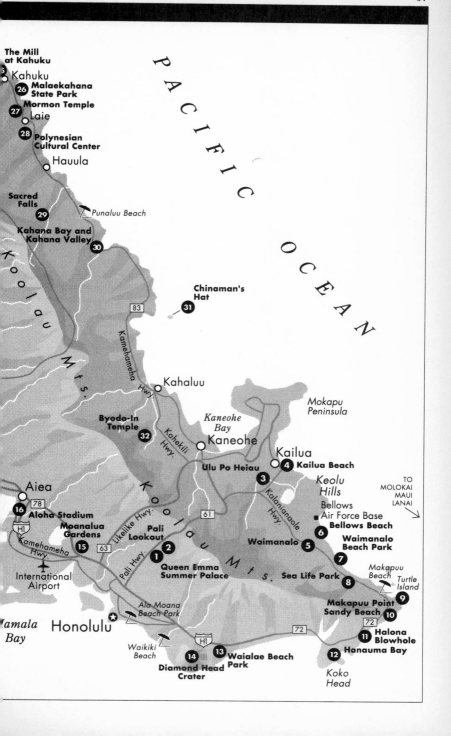

The Mill
at Kahuku

Kahuku

26 **Malaekahana
State Park**

Mormon Temple

27 Laie

28 **Polynesian
Cultural Center**

Hauula

**Sacred
Falls**

29

Punaluu Beach

**Kahana Bay and
Kahana Valley**

30

K o o l a u   M t s.

**Chinaman's
Hat**

31

P A C I F I C

O C E A N

83

Kamehameha Hwy.

Kahaluu

*Mokapu
Peninsula*

**Byodo-In
Temple**

32

Kahekili Hwy.

*Kaneohe
Bay*

Kaneohe

Kailua

Ulu Po Heiau

3

4 **Kailua Beach**

*Keolu
Hills*

Aiea

78

16

Aloha Stadium

**Moanalua
Gardens**

15

63

61

K o o l a u

Kalanianaole Hwy.

Bellows
Air Force Base

6 **Bellows Beach**

TO
MOLOKAI
MAUI
LANAI

H1

*Kamehameha
Hwy.*

**Pali
Lookout**

1 **2**

Waimanalo **5**

7

**Waimanalo
Beach Park**

M t s.

International
Airport

**Queen Emma
Summer Palace**

Pali Hwy.

Likelike Hwy.

Sea Life Park

8

*Makapuu
Beach*

*Turtle
Island*

9

*Ala Moana
Beach Park*

**Makapuu Point
Sandy Beach** **10**

*Mamala
Bay*

Honolulu

*Waikiki
Beach*

14

13

H1

**Waialae Beach
Park**

72

11

**Halona
Blowhole**

12 **Hanauma Bay**

**Diamond Head
Crater**

*Koko
Head*

72

Time Out Just past the entrance to Bellows Beach, on the makai side of the highway, is **Bueno Nalo** (41-865 Kalanianaole Hwy., tel. 808/259-7186), a funky Mexican eatery with fantastic south-of-the-border specialties at low prices. The space is small and unpretentious, but the food is terrific. It's BYOB; stop next door at Jimmy's Market if you'd like a cold one.

For dessert (if you're still hungry), go next door to **Ken's,** a no-frills bakery with delicious cinnamon rolls (tel. 808/259-9084).

❼ A block farther and you reach **Waimanalo Beach Park,** on the makai side of the road. The beach is safe for swimming, although the park area often draws young toughs (*see* Beaches Around Oahu, below).

❽ Another mile down the highway takes you to **Sea Life Park,** a marine attraction definitely worth a stop. Its finned menagerie includes the world's only "wholphin," the offspring of a romance between a whale and a dolphin. Children will especially enjoy watching dolphins leap and spin, penguins frolic, and a killer whale perform impressive tricks at the shows in the outdoor amphitheater. There's also an 11,000-gallon exhibit called "The Rocky Shores" recreating the surf-swept marine ecology of Hawaii's shoreline. The Pacific Whaling Museum teaches you about the fascinating history of whaling in Hawaii. Snacks and sodas are available, and there's a sit-down restaurant called The Galley. Even if you've seen trained cetaceans at other marine parks, the distinctively Hawaiian flavor makes this place special. The setting alone, right across from the ocean and Rabbit Island, is worth the price of admission. *Makapuu Point, Waimanalo, tel. 808/259-7933. Admission: $12.95 adults, $8.50 juniors 7–12, $4.50 children 4–6. Open Sat.–Thurs. 9:30–5, Fri. 9:30–10 PM. Live local music in the Galley Restaurant, Fri. 8:30 PM. Cost: $4.*

From the cliffs above Sea Life Park, colorful hang gliders often soar in the breezes. It takes a lot of daring to leap from these imposing heights, and there have been several fatalities here. Nestled in the cliff face above the water is the Makapuu Lighthouse (not open to the public).

Across the highway from Sea Life Park is **Makapuu Beach,** a beautiful cove that is great for seasoned bodysurfers but treacherous for the weak swimmer (*see* Beaches Around Oahu, below). Parking may be difficult to find, but the beach with offshore views of Rabbit Island makes a wonderful picnic spot. If you decide to keep going, the road winds up a hill, at the top of which is a pull-off on the makai side of the road. This is

❾ **Makapuu Point,** a fabulous photo opportunity, with breathtaking views of the mountains and bay, ocean and islands, including the large Rabbit Island and the smaller Turtle Island. The peninsula jutting out in the distance is Mokapu, site of a U.S. Marine base. The spired mountain peak is Mount Olomana. In front of you on the long pier is part of the Makai Undersea Test Range, a research facility that is closed to the public. The facility has launched a manned submersible to study Loihi, the active undersea volcano that is forming another Hawaiian island. Loihi should surface in about a thousand years.

Continue along the highway past the **Hawaii Kai Championship Golf Course** (tel. 808/395-2538), on the mauka side of the road (*see* Chapter 6). Across the highway is the area known as

Queen's Beach. In recent years, developers and conservationists have fought over the shoreline here. During the 1988 elections the people of Oahu voted to make it conservation land.

🔟 Next you'll see **Sandy Beach.** Tempting as this beach looks, it is not advisable to swim here. Notice that the only people in the water are local and young. They know the powerful and tricky waves well. Even so, the fierce shore break lands many of them in the hospital every year with back and neck injuries. The steady winds make Sandy Beach a popular place to fly kites (*see* Beaches Around Oahu, below).

Time Out Across Kalanianaole Highway from Sandy Beach is a fleet of **carryout trucks** offering fast-food specialties ideal for a break from the car. They're lined up along the shoulder, with colorful banners and enormous signs boasting their menus. On any given day they'll be selling shave ice (snow cones), plate lunches, cold sodas, and such dim sum goodies as *manapua* (dough wrapped around diced pork) and pork hash. Indulge yourself. You still have some traveling to do.

After Sandy Beach, the road takes you along the **Koko Head shoreline**—untamed and open to the ocean. This is a favorite stretch of coastline for visitors and residents alike, because the road twists and turns next to steep cliffs. Offshore, the islands of Molokai and Lanai call like distant sirens, and every once in a while, Maui is visible in blue silhouette. Pull into at least one scenic turnoff.

⓫ One stop features the famous **Halona Blowhole,** a lava tube that sucks in the ocean and then spits it out in lofty plumes. The blowhole may or may not perform, depending on the currents. Nearby is the tiny beach used to film the wave-washed love scene in *From Here to Eternity*. If you do get out here, lock up, because the spot is frequented by thieves.

⓬ Soon on the makai side of the road you will see a sign for **Hanauma Bay.** If you make only one stop during your drive, this one should be it. Even from the overlook, the horseshoe-shaped bay is a beauty, and you can easily see the reefs through the clear aqua waters. You can also see the crowds of people snorkeling and sunbathing, but it's still worth a visit (*see* Beaches Around Oahu, below, and Chapter 6).

From here back to Waikiki the highway passes several residential communities. First there is the sprawling **Hawaii Kai** development. Ancient Hawaiian fish ponds once flourished in this valley, but now the waterways are lined with suburban homes with two cars in the garage and a boat out back. The next communities are **Niu Valley** and **Aina Haina,** each of which has a small shopping center with a food store if you need a soda or a snack. Best to keep driving, however, because during rush hour, Kalanianaole Highway becomes choked with commuter traffic.

Right before you turn off from Kalanianaole Highway you'll notice a long stretch of green on the makai side. This is the private **Waialae Country Club** (4997 Kahala Ave., tel. 808/734–2151), scene of the annually televised Hawaiian Open golf tournament (*see* Chapter 6). Take the Kahala exit, right before the highway becomes the freeway. Turn left at the stoplight onto Kilauea Avenue. Here you'll see **Kahala Mall** (4211

Waialae Ave.), an upscale shopping complex with yuppie eateries, high-fashion stores, and five movie theaters.

Take a left on Hunakai Street and follow it to Kahala Avenue. If you want to hit one more beach, turn left and drive several blocks to **Waialae Beach Park,** where there is a shower house, beach pavilion, and nice sand for strolling. Windsurfers enjoy sailing here, though the reefs can be tricky. Just down the road is the fancy Kahala Hilton Hotel, where movie stars and royalty stay when they're in town.

Kahala Avenue takes you back toward Waikiki through **Kahala,** Oahu's wealthiest neighborhood. Here the oceanfront homes have lately been selling for more than $15 million, mostly to Japanese investors. At intervals along this tree-lined street are narrow lanes that provide public access to the beach.

As you reach a small, triangular park on the right, you have the option of continuing straight on what becomes Diamond Head Road or turning right on Monsarrat Avenue. A right turn will take you up to the top of a hill, where there is a sign pointing left to **Diamond Head Crater.** The famous extinct volcano got its common name from sailors who thought they had found precious gems on the slope; the diamonds proved to be volcanic refuse. If you're feeling energetic, drive through the tunnel to the inside of the crater and take the 40-minute (one-way) hike to the lookout at the top. From 760 feet, you'll get a tremendous view of where you've been and where you're going. *Monsarrat Ave. near 18th Ave., tel. 808/548–7455. Admission free. Open daily 6–6.*

If you continue straight along Diamond Head Road from the triangular park, you will crest a hill next to Diamond Head Crater. Pull off at one of the two scenic turnouts on the makai side of the road for a pretty view of the multicolored sails of the windsurfers below. A bit farther on the makai side is the picturesque **Diamond Head Lighthouse,** one of the oldest in the Pacific.

Drive along the road to Kapiolani Park, and stay on the right side of the park until you hit Kapahulu Avenue. Take a left, and you're back in Waikiki.

Tour 4: Circle Island Driving Tour

Numbers in the margin correspond with points of interest on the Oahu map.

Follow the directions to the H-1 Freeway heading west that appear at the beginning of the East Oahu Ring Tour. The freeway will diverge into Moanalua Freeway (Route 78). Stay on this past **Moanalua Gardens,** a lovely park with huge, spreading monkeypod trees. A hula festival is held on the ancient hula mound during the third weekend in July. Hikes are offered into historic Moanalua Valley; call for specific times. *1401 Mahiole, Honolulu, tel. 808/833–1944. Admission free. Open weekdays 8–4.*

On your left you'll pass **Aloha Stadium.** This 50,000-seat park has movable stands, and the seating configuration changes at the touch of a switch to conform to the type of event, be it a football or baseball game or a rock concert. There's no reason to stop here unless there's a game you plan to attend or, if you happen to see the unmistakable **Aloha Flea Market** in progress in the parking lot on a weekend. For 50¢ a head, Flea Market-goers can browse around the booths for hours. Operations range from slick tents with rows of neatly stacked, new wares to blankets spread on the pavement, covered with rusty tools and cracked china. You'll find gold trinkets, antique furniture, digital watches, Japanese fishing floats, T-shirts, muumuus, and palm-frond hats. Price haggling—in moderation—is the order of the day.

As you approach the stadium on the freeway, bear right at the sign to Aiea, then merge left onto Kamehameha Highway (Route 90) going south to Pearl Harbor. Turn right at the ⑰ Halawa Gate for a tour of the *Arizona* **Memorial**, a must-see stop. The gleaming white memorial shields the hulk of the USS *Arizona*, which sank with 1,102 men aboard when the Japanese attacked Pearl Harbor on December 7, 1941. The tour includes a 20-minute documentary and a shuttle-boat ride to the memorial. Afterward, you may also tour the USS *Bowfin*, a World War II submarine moored near the Visitor Center. You will be issued a "wand" for a self-guided tour that takes you through the vessel, including the torpedo room and engine room. *USS Arizona Memorial and Visitor Center, U.S. Naval Reservation, Pearl Harbor, tel. 808/422–0561. Admission free. Open daily 8–3. Tues. is the most crowded, with afternoon waits sometimes as long as 2 hours. Late in the week and early in the day are your best bets. For safety reasons, no children under 45 in. tall are permitted aboard the shuttle or the memorial. Also prohibited are people in bathing suits or with bare feet.*

After Pearl Harbor, retrace your steps and take either Kamehameha Highway or the H-2 Freeway to Wahiawa, home of the U.S. Army base at **Schofield Barracks.** This old plantation town has a distinctly military flavor.

Time Out   **Kemoo Farms** (1718 Wilikina Dr., Wahiawa, tel. 808/621–8481), a pleasant restaurant for lunch, is situated right on the main road in Wahiawa. Although there is no longer live music, this family-style, no-frills eatery on the shores of Lake Wilson still has a genuine feeling of aloha. It's closed Saturday.

If you're really into plants, stop by the **Wahiawa Botanical Gardens.** *1396 California Ave., Wahiawa, tel. 808/621–7321. Admission free. Open daily 9–4.*

For a modest glimpse of ancient Hawaiiana, take Kamehameha Highway, now Route 80, just over the bridge and turn onto the dirt road on the left. It's a short ride to the **Hawaiian Birth Stones,** once a sacred site for royal births.

Back on the main road, there is a scrubby-looking patch ambitiously called the **Del Monte Pineapple Variety Garden.** Unpromising as it looks, it's actually quite interesting, with varieties of the ubiquitous fruit ranging from thumb-size pink ones to big golden ones.

⑱ Turn left on Kamehameha Highway and you'll see the **Dole Pineapple Pavilion,** a big hit with Oahu sightseers since 1951. It has become even bigger with a new visitor pavilion, pineapple variety garden, 10,000-square-foot plantation gift shop, and restaurant. All of this, along with tram tours of an agricultural field, is a vast improvement over the old Dole Visitor Center.

64-1550 Kamehameha Hwy., tel. 808/621–8408. Admission free. Open daily 9–5:30.

From here, the road north cuts through acres of pineapple fields, followed by more acres of sugarcane. Once you hit the traffic circle, you have some choices to make. If you go around the circle and continue to **Mokuleia,** you'll come to the **polo fields** (*see* Chapter 6). Beyond that is the **Dillingham Airfield,** where you can watch the gliders or book a sailplane ride and try it yourself. *Glider Rides, Dillingham Airfield, Mokuleia, tel. 808/677–3404. Cost: $40 for one passenger, $60 for two. Open daily 10:30–5:30. No reservations, with 20-min flights every 20 minutes.*

Another option at the circle is to follow the signs to **Haleiwa,** a sleepy old plantation town that has come of age. In the 1920s it was a fashionable retreat at the end of a railroad line that no longer exists. During the '60s, the hippies gathered here. Now, Haleiwa is a fun mix of old and new. Old general stores peacefully coexist with contemporary boutiques and art galleries. Among the highlights are a pair of great fashion stores, **O'ogenesis** (66-249 Kamehameha Hwy., tel. 808/637–4580) and **RIX** (66-145 Kamehameha Hwy., tel. 808/637–9260). At a wonderful Haleiwa restaurant named **Jameson's by the Sea** (62-540 Kamehameha Hwy., tel. 808/637–4336), you can sit on the porch, sip a drink, and watch the boats go by.

Time Out   For a real slice of Haleiwa color, stop at **Matsumoto's** (66-087 Kamehameha Hwy., tel. 808/637–4827). Many sources claim that this place serves the best shave ice—a tropical snow cone, only better. They shave the ice right before your eyes and offer every flavor imaginable, including banana, mango, papaya, coconut, or combinations thereof. If you want to do it right, get it with vanilla ice cream and sweet azuki beans.

Leaving Haleiwa and continuing along Kamehameha Highway, you'll pass the famous north shore beaches, where the winter surf comes in size large. The first of these is **Waimea Bay,** a popular family picnic spot with a big, broad beach and fine facilities.

Across the street, on the mauka (mountain) side of the road, is **Waimea Falls Park.** An ancient Hawaiian community once thrived in Waimea Valley and today you can see remnants of that early civilization, as well as more than 2,500 species of flora from around the world. The garden trails are well marked, and the plants are labeled. An interesting assortment of animals roams the grounds, including the Hawaiian nene (goose), and there's a spectacular cliff-diving show at the 45-foot-high falls. Hawaiian games and dances are presented, there's a restaurant and picnic areas, and two evenings a month during the full moon, the park is open for free "moonwalks." *59-864 Kamehameha Hwy., Haleiwa, tel. 808/638–8511. Admission: $11.95 adults, $6.50 children 7–12, $2.25 children 4–6. Open daily 10–5:30.*

If you're interested in seeing a fine example of an ancient Hawaiian heiau (sacred stone platform for the worship of the gods), turn mauka (toward the mountains) at the Foodland store and take the Pupukea Road up the steep climb, not quite a mile, to the dirt road leading to the **Puu-o-Mahuka Heiau.** Once a site of human sacrifice, it is now on the National Register of Historic Places. The views are spectacular.

Continue along the coastal road past more famous surfing beaches, including **Ehukai** and **Sunset** (*see* Beaches Around Oahu, below). If it's wintertime, keep clear of those waves, which sometimes rise as high as 30 feet. Leave the sea to those daring (some say crazy) surfers who ride the towering waves with amazing grace.

24 The only hotel of any consequence in these parts is your next landmark: the **Turtle Bay Hilton** (57-091 Kamehameha Hwy., tel. 808/293–8811). If it's Sunday between 9 AM and 2 PM, you might want to stop for its incredibly extensive champagne brunch, served in a pretty oceanside dining room ($21 for adults, $11 for children under 12).

Time Out | Down the road from Turtle Bay is the **Amorient Aquaculture Stand,** a fascinating example of what has become an extremely successful venture for Oahu. Amorient (Kamehameha Hwy., Kahuku) is one of several companies that grow prawns, shrimp, and other fish and sea creatures in controlled environments. The results are as tasty as their natural counterparts. Stop by this stand on the makai side of the road and take a cup of carry-out shrimp cocktail to one of the picnic benches. The stand also sells fresh prawns, shrimp, and fish that you can take back to your condominium and cook for dinner.

Across the road, there is often a small lean-to set up with **Kahuku watermelons** for sale. By all means, buy one. They're the juiciest, sweetest melons you'll find on the Islands.

25 The old Kahuku Sugar Mill on Kamehameha Highway, which shut down in 1971 and then enjoyed a brief stint as a tourist attraction, has reopened as **The Mill at Kahuku** (56-565 Kamehameha Hwy., tel. 808/293–2414), with a restaurant and businesses. Visitors may take a free self-guided tour from 10 to 6 of parts of the turn-of-the-century mill, with its steam engines and enormous gears. There's also a gift shop and a craft area. The Country Kitchen Restaurant is open for breakfast, lunch, and dinner and serves a variety of American dishes.

26 As you approach the town of Laie, on the makai (ocean) side is a long stretch of pine trees. Look for the entrance to **Malaekahana State Park,** a lovely place to take a break from driving. You can park in the big lot and wander the shady grounds or stroll on the long beach. At low tide you can even wade to Goat Island. *Admission free. Open Oct.–Mar. 7–6:45; Apr.–Sept. 7–7:45.*

27 Coming up on the makai side is a road that leads to the **Mormon Temple** (55-415 Iosepa St., tel. 808/293–9167), a white structure made of pulverized volcanic rock and coral. It is a house of worship, not a visitor attraction. The Mormons run Brigham Young University's Hawaii campus, in Laie as well.

28 The Mormons also operate the sprawling **Polynesian Cultural Center,** next on the makai side of the road. A visit to the center isn't cheap, but it's worth the money to see the 40 acres of lagoons and seven re-created South Pacific villages representing Hawaii, Tahiti, Samoa, Fiji, the Marquesas, New Zealand, and Tonga. Shows and demonstrations enliven the area, and there's a spectacular evening dinner show. If you're short on time, you can try to sandwich this attraction into a driving tour, though you'll miss much of what makes it so popular. If you're staying in Honolulu, it's better to see the center as part of a van tour, so you won't have to drive home after the evening show. *55-370 Kamehameha Hwy., Laie, tel. 808/293-3333 or 808/923-1861. Cost: Standard Package (general admission to all villages and daytime shows plus American dinner) $38.95 adults, $19.95 children 5–11. Luau Package (general admission, afternoon shows, and the luau) $44.95 adults, $25.95 children 5–11. Ambassador Passport (this VIP ticket includes standard shows and attractions, plus a kukui-nut-lei greeting, an escorted tour, a special dinner, prime show seating, and more) $69.95 adults, $44.95 children 5–11. Open Mon.–Sat. 12:30–12:30.*

㉙ About 4 miles down the highway on the mauka (toward the mountains) side of the road, look for the Hawaii Visitors Bureau sign for **Sacred Falls.** This wild state park, with a strenuous 2-mile hike to an 80-foot-high waterfall, is Hawaiian country as you dreamed it would be. A swim in the pool beneath the falls is a welcome refresher after the hike. Be sure to hike with someone else, and don't attempt the trail if there has been rain; the valley is subject to flash flooding, and the trail can be slippery. *Admission free. Open Oct.–Mar., daily 7–6:45; Apr.–Sept., daily 7–7:45.*

㉚ A bit farther down the road you'll pass **Kahana Bay** and **Kahana Valley,** where ancient Hawaiians once lived. Don't bother stopping here; the water is too shallow for decent swimming, and the valley is not safe for hiking during hunting season.

The next thing to look for, although it's not spectacular, is the **Crouching Lion** mountain formation on the ridge line behind an inn of the same name. If someone tells you it has a deeply significant Hawaiian legend attached to it, don't believe them. The lion was an idea thought up by modern-day promoters. As you continue driving along the shoreline, you'll notice a picturesque little island called, for obvious reasons, **Chinaman's Hat.**
㉛

㉜ At the town of Waiahole is a little market with an unlikely name, Hygienic Store. Here you can branch off the Kahekili Highway (Route 83) and head for the Valley of the Temples and its lovely **Byodo-In Temple.** This replica of a 900-year-old temple in Kyoto, Japan, dramatically set against the sheer green cliffs of the Koolau Mountains, is surrounded by Japanese gardens and a two-acre lake stocked with prize carp. A two-ton statue of Buddha presides over all. *47-200 Kahekili Hwy., Kaneohe, tel. 808/239-8811. Admission: $2 adults, $1 children under 12. Open daily 8–4:30.*

Continue on Kahekili Highway to the Likelike Highway, where you turn mauka and head back toward Honolulu through the Wilson Tunnel. The highway leads to the Lunalilo Freeway going east. Exit at Pali Highway and go south through downtown Honolulu to Nimitz Highway, then turn left on Ala Moana Boulevard, which leads to Kalakaua Avenue in Waikiki.

Off the Beaten Track

Dole Cannery Square. Oahu boasts the biggest pineapple in the world, weighing in at 28.5 tons and standing 199.3 feet tall, with 46 leaves sticking out of its crown. This mega-pineapple is actually a 100,000-gallon water tower built in 1928 by Hawaii

Pineapple Company, the predecessor to Dole. More important, it marks the location of the cannery, at whose visitor center you can learn all about the century-old business history of Hawaii's fruit export. The center has a 27-projector film, exhibits, specialty shops, a food court, and a fascinating factory tour lasting 35 minutes. Complimentary Dole products are served at the end of the tour. *650 Iwilei Rd., Honolulu, tel. 808/531–8855. Free "Pineapple Transit" buses leave from Waikiki hotels on a regular schedule; ask at your hotel front desk for times. Entrance to the square is free; admission to tour and film, $5 adults and children 13–17. There are continuous cannery tours daily every 15 min, 9–4.*

Maui Divers' Jewelry Design Center. The folks who run this attraction like to say they'll take you "40 fathoms in five languages." Intrigued? Then stop by this center to discover how Hawaii's official state gemstone—coral—is mined. The 30-year-old company presents the story of coral in state-of-the-art video theaters. Then you move on to the manufacturing exhibit area, where goldsmiths and artisans make new jewelry designs, cut and polish coral, and set it with diamonds before your very eyes. In the last room the finished products are on display and for sale. *1520 Liona St., Honolulu, tel. 808/946–7979. Tours weekdays 10–3. Closed Sun. Complimentary shuttle bus transportation available from Waikiki. By car from Waikiki, take the Ala Wai Canal to Kalakaua Ave. and turn right. Turn left on Beretania, left on Keeaumoku, and left on Liona. By public transportation, take the No. 2 bus from Waikiki, get off at the corner of Beretania and Keeaumoku, and walk 3 blocks makai (toward the ocean) to Liona.*

Senator Fong's Plantation and Gardens. Though Fong hasn't been a senator for more than a dozen years, this enterprising 83-year-old ex-legislator hosts an agricultural attraction showcasing the splendors of Hawaii's rich soil and climate. Flowering vines, ethnic gardens, edible bushes, and tropical fruit trees cover 725 acres of windward Oahu. Guests get a 40-minute guided tour of the plantation and gardens in an open-air minibus. The visitor center includes a snack bar, rest rooms, and a gift shop. *47-285 Pulama Rd., Kahaluu, tel. 808/239–6775. Admission: $6.50 adults, $3 children 5–12. Open daily 9–4. 35 min from Honolulu on the way to the Polynesian Cultural Center, 2 mi past Byodo-In Temple.*

Beaches Around Oahu

Here is an alphabetical listing of some of the finer beaches scattered around Oahu's shores.

Ala Moana Beach Park. Waikiki aside, this is the most popular beach for tourists. Residents love Ala Moana as well, because it features a protective reef, which keeps the waters calm. The sand is hard and packed, and bodies are everywhere, tanning, listening to radios, practicing acrobatics, eating picnics, and watching the surf action outside the reef. To the Waikiki side is a peninsula called Magic Island, with picnic tables, shady trees, and paved sidewalks ideal for jogging. Ala Moana also features playing fields, changing houses, indoor and outdoor showers, lifeguards, concession stands, and tennis courts. This is a beach for everyone; don't expect to find easy parking on the weekends. *Honolulu, makai side of Ala Moana Shopping Cen-*

ter and Ala Moana Blvd. For public transportation from Waikiki, take the No. 8 bus, get off at the shopping center, and walk across Ala Moana Blvd.

Bellows Field Beach. Locals come here for the fine swimming on the weekends, when the Air Force opens the beach to civilians. The waves are great for bodysurfing, and the sand is soft for sunbathing. There are showers, abundant parking, and plenty of places for picnicking underneath shady ironwood trees. There are no food concessions here, but right outside the entrance gate is a McDonald's and some other carryouts. *Entrance is on Kalanianaole Hwy., near Waimanalo town center. It is marked with signs on the makai side of the road. Open to the public on weekends and holidays.*

Ehukai Beach Park. Ehukai is part of a series of beaches running for many miles along the north shore. There's a grassy area above the beach and a steep dune dropping down to it. The long, wide, and generally uncrowded beach has a changing house with showers and an outdoor shower and water fountain. Bring along a cooler with sodas, as there is virtually no shade here, and the nearest store is a mile away. The winter waves are fierce, and the lifeguards are constantly warning people to be careful. Right offshore is the famous Banzai Pipeline, site of international surfing competitions. *North shore, 1 mi north of the Foodland store at Pupukea. Turn makai off Kamehameha Hwy. onto the dirt road that parallels the highway. The small Ehukai parking lot is about 2 blocks away.*

Haleiwa Beach Park. The winter waves are impressive here, but in the summertime the ocean is like a lake, ideal for family swimming. The beach itself is big and pleasant and often full of locals. Broad lawns between the highway and the beach are busy with volleyball action, Frisbee games, and groups of barbecuers. There is a changing house with showers. No food concession, but Haleiwa has everything you need for provisions. *North shore, makai side of Kamehameha Hwy., north of Haleiwa town center and just past the boat harbor.*

Hanauma Bay. Crowds flock to this horseshoe-shaped, palm-lined, sunken crater rimmed with a long, narrow crescent of packed sand. The main attraction here is the snorkeling, and the coral reefs are clearly visible through the turquoise waters. Beyond the reef is a popular site for scuba-diving classes. The bay is best early in the morning (7 AM), before the crowds arrive. There is a busy food concession on the beach, plus changing houses and indoor and outdoor showers. *Makai of Kalanianaole Hwy., at the top of the hill just east of Hawaii Kai. A big sign points to the parking lot. A jitney runs down the steep slope to the beach for 50¢, one-way. The Hanauma Bay Shuttle Service (tel. 808/737-6188) runs to and from Waikiki and costs $1.50 each way.*

Kahana Bay Beach Park. Parents often bring their children to wade in safety at this pretty beach cove with very shallow, protected waters. A grove of tall ironwood and pandanus trees keeps the area cool, shady, and ideal for a picnic. There are changing houses, showers, and picnic tables. An ancient Hawaiian fish pond, which was in use until the 1920s, is visible nearby. Across the highway is Kahana Valley, burgeoning with banana, breadfruit, and mango trees. *On the windward side of* *the island, makai of Kamehameha Hwy., just north of Kualoa Park.*

Kualoa Regional Park. Grassy expanses border a long, narrow stretch of beach with spectacular views of Kaneohe Bay and the Koolau Mountains. The highlight of the landscape/seascape is an islet called Mokoli'i (more commonly known as Chinaman's Hat), which rises like the cone-shaped headgear 206 feet above the water. At low tide you can wade out to the island on the reef. This is without doubt one of the island's most beautiful picnic, camping, and beach areas. The one drawback is that it's usually windy. Bring a cooler; no refreshments are sold here. There are places to shower, change, and picnic in the shade of palm trees. *On the windward side, makai of Kamehameha Hwy., just north of Waiahole.*

Kailua Beach Park. Steady breezes attract windsurfers by the dozens to this long, palm-fringed beach with gently sloping sands. You can rent equipment in Kailua and try it yourself (*see* Chapter 6). Young athletes and members of the military enjoy this beach, as do local families, so it gets pretty crowded on the weekend. There are showers, changing houses, picnic areas, and a concession stand. You can also buy your picnic provisions at the Kalapawai Market nearby. *On the windward side, makai of Kailua town. Turn right on Kailua Rd. at the market, cross a bridge, then turn left into the beach parking lot.*

Makaha Beach Park. Tourists generally don't visit the 20-mile stretch of the Waianae coast because it has just one hotel, the Sheraton Makaha. It features a string of beaches where the swimming is generally decent in the summer, and the scene is much more local than in Honolulu. At Makaha Beach, families string up tarps for the day, unload hibachis, set up lawn chairs, get out the fishing gear, and strum ukuleles while they "talk story," or chat. This quarter-mile-long beach has a changing house and showers and is the site of a yearly big-board surf meet (*see* Chapter 6). *On the Waianae coast, 1½ hours west of Honolulu on the H-1 Fwy. and Farrington Hwy. On the makai side of the highway.*

Makapuu Beach. This tiny crescent cove at the base of high sea cliffs is a gem of a sunbathing spot. From the beach you can see Rabbit Island, a picturesque cay so named because some say it looks like a swimming rabbit. If you look up you might see a hang glider who has just launched from the cliffs above. Swimming at Makapuu should be reserved for strong strokers and bodysurfers, because the swells can be big and powerful here. Makapuu is a popular beach with the locals. Because the lot is small, parking can be tricky, and you may have to park on the narrow shoulder and walk down to the beach. There is a changing house with indoor and outdoor showers. *Makai of Kalanianaole Hwy., across from Sea Life Park, 2 mi south of Waimanalo.*

Malaekahana Beach Park. Families love to camp here, because there are groves of ironwood trees that provide lots of shade and breezes during the heat of the day. The beach itself is fairly narrow but long enough for a 20-minute stroll, one-way. The waves are never too big to swim in, and sometimes they're just right for the beginning bodysurfer. At low tide, you can wade out to tiny Goat Island, just offshore, and the water never gets much more than waist high. If you decide to wade, be sure to wear sneakers so you don't stub your toe on a rock. There are several changing houses and indoor and outdoor showers, plus picnic tables. *On the windward side. Entrance gates are makai of Kamehameha Hwy., ½ mi north of Laie. They're easy to miss, because you can't see the beach from the road.*

Sandy Beach. There's generally a rescue truck parked on the road by Sandy's, which means that people are swimming where they shouldn't and hurting themselves. The shore break is mean here, but that doesn't stop young men and women from jumping in. It should, however, stop *you* unless you are a strong swimmer. Sandy's is a popular spot for the high school and college crowd. Due to the strong, steady winds, it is a kite-flyer's paradise. There's a changing house with indoor and outdoor showers here, and food trucks across the highway. *Makai of Kalanianaole Hwy., 2 mi east of Hanauma Bay.*

Sunset Beach. This is another link in the chain of north shore beaches, which extends for miles. Sunset has a tiny parking lot, so it's easy to miss. It is popular for its gentle summer waves and crashing winter surf. The beach is broad, and the sand is soft. It's a fun place to look for puka shells. Across the street there are usually carryout trucks selling shave ice, plate lunches, and sodas. No facilities except a portable outhouse. *On the north shore, 1 mi north of Ehukai Beach Park, on the makai side of Kamehameha Hwy.*

Waimanalo Beach Park. The lawn at Waimanalo plays host to hundreds of local people who set up minicamps for the day, complete with hibachis, radios, lawn chairs, coolers, and shade tarps. Sometimes these folks are not very friendly to tourists. However, the beach itself is more welcoming, and from here you can walk a mile along the shore for fantastic windward and mountain views. Boogie boarders and bodysurfers enjoy the predictably gentle waves of this beach. The grassy, shady grounds have picnic tables and shower houses. *On the windward side. Look for the signs makai of Kalanianaole Hwy., just south of Waimanalo town.*

Waimea Bay. Made popular in that old Beach Boys song, "Surfin' U.S.A.," Waimea Bay is a slice of hang-ten heaven. Winter is when you should stand well away from the shore break and leave the 25-foot-high waves to the hotdogs. Try walking near the water and the lifeguards will shoo you away through their bullhorns. Summer is the time to swim and snorkel in the calm waters. The beach is a broad crescent of soft sand, backed by a shady area with tables, a changing house, and showers. Parking is almost impossible in the lot on weekends, so folks just park along the road and walk down. *On the north shore. Across the street from Waimea Falls Park, 3 mi north of Haleiwa, on the makai side of Kamehameha Hwy.*

Yokohama Bay. This Waianae-coast beach at the very end of the road feels remote and untouched, which may explain its lack of crowds. Locals come here to fish and swim in waters that are calm enough for children during the summer. Bring provisions, because the nearest town is a 15-minute drive away. The beach is narrow, and rocky in places. There's a changing house and showers, plus a small parking lot, but most folks just pull over and park on the side of the bumpy road. *On the Waianae coast, at the northern end of Farrington Hwy., about 7 mi north of Makaha.*

5 Shopping

Locals used to complain about the lack of shopping options in the Islands. Some even went so far as to hop on a plane and fly to the mainland to find the latest fashions or that perfect gift. Happily, those days are past, and Hawaii (particularly Oahu) has assumed its place as an international crossroads of the shopping scene.

As the capital of the 50th state, Honolulu is the number-one shopping town in the Islands. It features sprawling shopping malls, spiffy boutiques, hotel stores, family-run businesses, and a variety of other enterprises selling brand-new merchandise as well as priceless antiques and one-of-a-kind souvenirs and gifts. What makes shopping on Oahu so interesting is the unusual cultural diversity of its products and the many items unique to Hawaii.

As you drive around the island, you'll find souvenir stands and what appear to be discount stores for island products. Watch out, because you could end up buying something tacky and expensive. Start with the reliable stores listed below; they're bound to have what you're looking for, and a little extra.

Major shopping malls are generally open daily from 10 to 9, although some shops may close at 4 or 5.

Shopping Centers

Oahu's many fine shopping malls assemble a little of everything at a wide range of prices. Be sure to wander to the upper levels, where the rents are cheaper and the shops are usually smaller and more original.

In Waikiki   **The Royal Hawaiian Shopping Center** (2201 Kalakaua Ave., tel. 808/922–0588), fronting the Royal Hawaiian and Sheraton Waikiki hotels, is three blocks long and contains 120 stores on three levels. There are such Paris shops as **Chanel** (tel. 808/923–0255) and **Louis Vuitton** (tel. 808/926–0621), as well as local arts and crafts from the **Little Hawaiian Craft Shop** (tel. 808/926–2662), which features Bishop Museum reproductions, Niihau shell leis (those super-expensive leis from the island of Niihau), feather hat bands, and South Pacific art. **Bijoux Jewelers** (tel. 808/926–1088) has a fun collection of baubles, bangles, and beads for your perusal. The **Friendship Store** (tel. 808/926–1255), one of the few Chinese government stores outside mainland China, showcases Chinese arts and crafts, from baskets to fine rugs. The **Accessory Tree** (tel. 808/922–6595) carries an assortment of belts, bags, and jewelry, some crafted from shells, others hand-painted, plus a limited selection of clothing.

The Waikiki Shopping Plaza (2270 Kalakaua Ave., tel. 808/923–1191) is across the street; its landmark is a 75-foot-high water-sculpture gizmo, which looks great when it's working. Two clothing shops worth checking out are **Chocolates for Breakfast** (tel. 808/923–4426), with its trendy, fairly expensive items from the high-fashion scene; and its sister store, **Villa Roma** (tel. 808/923–4447), equally trendy but younger and less pricey. There's a **Waldenbooks** and "Voyage," a show featuring Polynesian song and dance, at 6:45 and 8:30 PM, on the fourth floor.

The Waikiki Trade Center (at the corner of Kuhio and Seaside Aves., tel. 808/922–7444) is slightly out of the action and features shops only on the first floor. Included are such prizes as

It's Only a Paper Moon (tel. 808/924–8521), with greeting cards that go beyond the usual Hallmark variety. **Bebe's Boutique** (tel. 808/926–7888), which leans to the leather look, is for the slim and affluent. **C. June Shoes** (tel. 808/926–1574) offers European designer shoes, clothing, handbags, belts, and accessories, featuring Carlo Fiori of Italy.

Waikiki also boasts three theme-park-style shopping centers. Right in the heart of the area is the **International Market Place** (2330 Kalakaua Ave., tel. 808/923–9871), a tangle of souvenir stalls under a giant banyan tree. It spills into adjacent **Kuhio Mall** (2301 Kuhio Ave., tel. 808/922–2724), which has more of the same beads, beach towels, and shirts. **King's Village** (131 Kaiulani Ave., tel. 808/944–6855) looks like a Hollywood stage set of monarchy-era Honolulu, complete with a changing-of-the-guard ceremony every evening at 6:15.

Around Honolulu **Ala Moana Shopping Center** (1450 Ala Moana Blvd., tel. 808/946–2811) is a gigantic open-air mall just five minutes from Waikiki on the No. 8 bus. The 50-acre center is on the corner of Atkinson and Ala Moana boulevards. All the main Hawaiian department stores are here, including **Sears** (tel. 808/947–0211) and **J. C. Penney** (tel. 808/946–8068). **Liberty House** (tel. 808/941–2345) is highly recommended for its selection of stylish Hawaiian wear, and high fashion is available at **Chocolates for Breakfast** (tel. 808/947–3434). For stunning Hawaiian prints, try the **Art Board** (tel. 808/946–4863), and buy your local footwear at the **Slipper House** (tel. 808/949–0155).

Also at Ala Moana is **Shirokiya** (tel. 808/941–9111), an authentic Japanese department store where someone is usually demonstrating the latest state-of-the-art kitchen gadget in at least two languages, one of them Japanese. The upper-level food section is like a three-ring circus of free samples, hawkers, and strange Japanese specialties, both fresh and tinned. The toy department whirls and clinks with windup wonders.

Ala Moana also features a huge assortment of local-style souvenir shops, such as **Hawaiian Island Creations** (tel. 808/941–4491) and **Irene's Hawaiian Gifts** (tel. 808/946–6818). Its **Makai Market** is a food bazaar, with central seating and 20 kitchens serving everything from pizza to health food, poi, ribs, sushi, and Thai food. Stores open their doors daily between 7 and 9:30 AM. The shopping center closes weekdays at 9 PM; Saturday it closes at 5:30, and Sunday at 5, with longer hours during the Christmas holidays.

Heading west, toward downtown Honolulu, you'll run into **Ward Centre** (1200 Ala Moana Blvd., tel. 808/531–6411) and **Ward Warehouse** (1050 Ala Moana Blvd., tel. 808/531–1611). Both are eclectic mixes of boutiques and restaurants. Two of their best-loved shops are **Thongs 'N Things** (tel. 808/524–8229), notable for its huge collection of casual footwear, and **Neon Leon** (tel. 808/545–7666), which features racks and racks of outrageous notecards.

Farther west awaits **Waterfront Plaza** (500 Ala Moana Blvd. between South and Punchbowl Sts., tel. 808/538–1441), a new conglomeration of fun retailers and eateries. Be sure to stop by **Nothing You Need** (tel. 808/533–0029), an ultra-high-tech shop of electronic toys, gadgets, and gizmos.

Kahala Mall (4211 Waialae Ave., tel. 808/732–7736) is located 10 minutes by car from Waikiki in the chic residential neighborhood of Kahala, near the slopes of Diamond Head. This mall features such upscale clothing stores as **Liberty House** (tel. 808/ 941–2345; *see* listing in Ala Moana Shopping Center, above) and **Carol & Mary** (tel. 808/926–1264), which offers high-level fashions for those evenings out. **Reyn's** (tel. 808/737–8313) is the acknowledged place to go for men's resort wear; its aloha shirts have muted colors and button-down collars, suitable for most social occasions. Along with a fun assortment of gift shops, Kahala Mall also features eight movie theaters (tel. 808/735– 9744) for post-shopping entertainment.

Specialty Stores

Aloha Shirts and Muumuus
For stylish Hawaiian wear, the kind worn by local men and women, look in **Liberty House** at 2314 Kalakaua Avenue, and other locations throughout the Islands; **Carol & Mary,** at the Halekulani and Hilton Hawaiian Village hotels; and **Andrade,** at the Royal Hawaiian and King's Village shopping centers as well as at the Hyatt Regency Waikiki, Princess Kaiulani, Royal Hawaiian, Sheraton Moana Surfrider, and Sheraton Waikiki hotels. If you want something bright, bold, and cheap, there are any number of "garment factory to you" outlets and street stalls. Don't bother with free buses that offer to take you to a factory. They're a waste of limited vacation time and the factory bargains aren't exceptional. For vintage aloha shirts try **Bailey's Antique Clothing and Thrift Shop** (758 Kapahulu Ave.), just beyond Waikiki.

High Fashion
Liberty House is again recommended. **Carol & Mary** has been known for high quality and designer labels since 1937. **Altillo** (2117 Kuhio Ave. and a new location in Kahala Mall) carries a line of European menswear, with shirts ranging from $20 to over $200. **Chocolates for Breakfast,** in the Waikiki Shopping Plaza, is the trendy end of the high fashion scene. For the latest in shoes and bags, **C. June Shoes,** in the Waikiki Trade Center, displays an elegant array of unusual and *expensive* styles. **Mosaic,** on the 10th floor of the Waikiki Business Plaza, just across the street from the Waikiki Shopping Plaza, is a wholesale outlet open to the public. It carries the Mosaic line along with a few other "name" labels. On the same floor, **Leathers of the Sea** has the best prices on eel-skin purses, wallets, and attaché cases.

Resort Wear Clothing
Liberty House has the widest selection. **Chapman's** at the Sheraton Waikiki, Hyatt Regency Waikiki, Royal Hawaiian, Sheraton Moana Surfrider, Ikikai Waikiki, and Hilton Hawaiian Village hotels and other island locations, is a fine men's specialty shop. **McInerny** has a couple of theme shops and a clearance shop in the Royal Hawaiian Shopping Center. **Andrade** has a compact but good inventory of both men's and women's resort fashions in its hotel shops.

Mature women who like clothing that is conservative and well-designed absolutely rave about **Alfred Shaheen** fashions. See for yourself. They're at the Royal Hawaiian Shopping Center, Rainbow Bazaar, King's Village, Hyatt Regency Waikiki, Ilikai Waikiki, and Sheraton Waikiki.

Food
Take home fresh pineapple, papaya, or coconut. Jam comes in flavors like poha, passion fruit, and guava. Kona coffee has an international following. There are lines of dried food products

such as *saimin* (Japanese noodle soup), *haupia* (a firm coconut pudding), and teriyaki barbecue sauce. All kinds of cookies are available, as well as exotic teas, drink mixes, and pancake syrups. And don't forget the macadamia nuts. By law, all fresh-fruit products must be inspected by the Department of Agriculture. The following stores carry only inspected fruit, ready for shipment:

The best place to shop for all these delicacies is the second floor of **F. W. Woolworth** (2225 Kalakaua Ave., tel. 808/923–2331). It accepts credit-card (MC, V) telephone orders and ships directly to your home. So do **ABC stores,** with 24 locations in Waikiki (tel. 808/538–6743; MC, V). An outfit called **Fresh From Hawaii** (2270 Kalakaua Ave., Suite 1514, tel. 808/922–5077) specializes in inspected, packed pineapple and papaya, plus gift packs of jams and Kona coffee. It will deliver to your hotel and to the airport baggage check-in counter or ship to the mainland United States and Canada. It also has concessions inside Woolworth's, at the Royal Hawaiian Shopping Center, International Market Place, Outrigger Waikiki Hotel, and Outrigger Reef Hotel; telephone credit-card orders are also accepted (MC, V).

Gifts **Mandalay,** in the Halekulani Hotel (2199 Kalia Rd.), goes in for the ethnic look with lots of Thai imports, caftans, kimonos, exclusive men's shirts, and Issey Miyake designs. Also at the Halekulani, **Takenoya Arts** specializes in intricately carved netsuke (small Japanese ornaments), both antique and contemporary, and one-of-a-kind ivory necklaces, some reasonably priced.

Hawaiian Arts and Crafts One of the nicest gifts is something handcrafted of native Hawaiian wood. Some species of trees grow only in Hawaii. Koa and milo each have a beautiful color and grain. The great koa forests are disappearing because of environmental factors, so the wood is becoming valuable. There are also framed arrangements of delicate *limu* (seaweed), feather leis and polished kukui nut leis, wooden bowls, and hula implements.

The best selection and best prices are at the **Little Hawaiian Craft Shop** in the Royal Hawaiian Shopping Center. The manager is a former librarian and enjoys talking about the ancient arts. Some items are Bishop Museum reproductions, with a portion of the profits going to the museum. The shop also has a good selection of Niihau shell leis (those superexpensive leis from Niihau Island), feather hatbands, and South Pacific arts. Both traditional Hawaiian and more contemporary arts and crafts are featured at the **Kuhio Mall Craft Court.** It's upstairs and hard to find but worth the search. Usually you'll find several artists at work. Prices are reasonable.

Jewelry You can buy gold chains by the inch on the street corner, and jade and coral trinkets by the dozen. **Bernard Hurtig's** has a fine jewelry department, specializing in 18K gold and antique jade. Hurtig's boutique jewelry is a collection of fabulous fakes, many of them reproductions of famous pieces and priced from $35. Hurtig's is a recognized authority on *netsuke,* the small Japanese sword ornaments carved in jade, ivory, and other precious materials. Waikiki shops are at the Kahala Hilton Hotel (5000 Kahala Ave.) and Hilton Hawaiian Village (2005 Kalia Rd.). **Haimoff & Haimoff Creations in Gold,** located in the Halekulani Hotel (2199 Kalia Rd.), features the original work of award-winning jewelry designer Harry Haimoff.

6 Sports

Participant Sports

Biking

The good news is that the coastal roads are flat and well paved. On the downside, they're also awash in vehicular traffic. Frankly, biking is no fun in either Waikiki or Honolulu, but things are a bit better outside the city. Be sure to take along a nylon jacket for the frequent showers on the windward side and remember that Hawaii is Paradise After the Fall: Lock your bike, or be prepared to hike.

Mountain bikes are available for rent at **Aloha Funway Rentals** (1778 and 1984 Kalakaua Ave., Waikiki, tel. 808/942–9696 and 947–4579). Day rate: $12.95 for a 10-speed. You can buy a bike or, if you brought your own, you can get it repaired at **Eki Cyclery Shop** (1603 Dillingham Blvd., Honolulu, tel. 808/847–2005). If you want to find some biking buddies, write ahead to the **Hawaii Bicycling League** (Box 4403, Honolulu 96813, tel. 808/988–7175). This organization can tell you about upcoming races, which are frequent on all the Islands.

Fitness Centers

Clark Hatch Physical Fitness Center has complete weight-training facilities, an indoor pool, a racquetball court, aerobics classes, treadmills, and indoor running apparatus. *745 Fort St., Honolulu, tel. 808/536–7205. Daily, weekly, and monthly guest rates work out to approximately $7 a day. Open weekdays 6 AM—8 PM, Sat. 7:30 AM—5:30 PM.*

World Gym is Waikiki's most accessible fitness center. In fact, 80% of its business comes from tourists. Full free-weight facilities, Nautilus machines, Universal gyms, and a pro shop are open to men and women. *1701 Ala Wai Blvd., Honolulu, tel. 808/942–8171. $9 a day, $35 a week, $50 for 2 weeks. Open daily 24 hrs.*

Among the hotels that have established fitness centers are the following:

Halekulani Hotel (2199 Kalia Rd., Waikiki, tel. 808/923–2311) has aerobics classes three times a week. Universal weight machines, a treadmill, two exercise bikes, and a massage room are available, for guests only.

Hilton Hawaiian Village (2005 Kalia Rd., Waikiki, tel. 808/949–4321) has an extensive fitness center open to those staying in the hotel's Alii Tower, including a Nautilus weight room and a Jacuzzi.

Kahala Hilton (5000 Kahala Ave., Kahala, tel. 808/734–2211) has an excellent, sophisticated fitness center available for its guests. The hotel is affiliated with Maunalua Bay Club, which has tennis courts, a swimming pool, aerobics classes, Nautilus machines, rowing machines, and treadmills. The Kahala offers a shuttle to the club, which is only five minutes away from the hotel.

Golf

Oahu is honeycombed with golf holes. It has more golf courses than any other Hawaiian Island—more than two dozen—most of them open to the public. One of the most popular facilities is the **Ala Wai Golf Course** (404 Kapahulu Ave., tel. 808/296–4653) on Waikiki's mauka (north) end, across the Ala Wai Canal. It's par 70 on approximately 6,424 yards and has a pro shop and a restaurant. Greens fees: $18 weekdays; $20 weekends and holidays; carts $11. The waiting list is long, so if you plan to play, call the minute you land.

You'll stand a better chance of getting to play at the 6,350-yard **Hawaii Kai Championship Course** or the neighboring 2,386-yard **Hawaii Kai Executive Course** (8902 Kalanianaole Hwy., Honolulu, tel. 808/395–2358 for either). Fees are $50 with a cart for the former and $17.50 with a cart for the latter. Another good buy is the **Olomana Golf Links** on the windward side (41–1801 Kalanianaole Hwy., Waimanolo, tel. 808/259–7926). Fees, including carts, are $39 weekdays, $49 weekends and holidays. The **Sheraton Makaha Resort and Country Club** has an exceptional course in a beautiful valley setting (84–626 Makaha Valley Rd., Waianae, tel. 808/695–9544). Rates, including cart: $45 for guests, $95 for nonguests. The 18-hole golf course at the **Turtle Bay Hilton** (57–091 Kamehameha Hwy., Kahuku, tel. 808/293–8811) costs $65 for hotel guests, $80 weekdays, $90 weekends for nonguests, with cart.

Horseback Riding

Kualoa Ranch (49–560 Kamehameha Hwy., Kaaawa, tel. 808/237–8515; in Honolulu, tel. 808/538–7636), on the windward side, across from Kualoa Beach Park, features trail rides in Kaaawa, one of the most beautiful valleys in all Hawaii. (Cost: $20 per hour.) It also has an activities club. For $90 a day, you can go horseback riding, fly in a helicopter, ride a dune buggy, go snorkeling, try the shooting range, and have lunch (weekdays only). **Sheraton Makaha Lio Stables** (Box 896, Waianae, tel. 808/695–9511 ext. 7646) offers escorted rides into Makaha Valley; a one-hour guided trail ride costs $18.50 per person, and sunset rides are available. **Turtle Bay Hilton** (57–091 Kamehameha Hwy., Kahuku, tel. 808/293–8811) has 75 acres of hotel property (including a private beach) for exploring on horseback, at $21 per guest, $23 per nonguest, per 45 minutes.

Jogging

In Honolulu, the most popular places are the two parks, **Kapiolani** and **Ala Moana,** at either end of Waikiki. In both cases, the loop around the park is just under 2 miles. You can also run a 4.6-mile ring around **Diamond Head Crater,** past scenic views, luxurious homes, and herds of other joggers. If you jog along the 1.5-mile **Ala Wai Canal,** you'll probably glimpse outrigger-canoe teams practicing on the canal. If you're looking for jogging companions, show up for the free **Honolulu Marathon Clinic** that starts at the Kapiolani Park Bandstand (Mar.–Nov., Sun. 7:30 AM).

Once you leave Honolulu, it gets trickier to find places to jog that are scenic as well as safe. Best to stick to the well-traveled routes, or ask the experienced folks at the **Running Room** (559 Kapahulu Ave., Honolulu, tel. 808/737–2422) for advice.

Tennis

In the Waikiki area there are four free public courts at **Kapiolani Tennis Courts** (2748 Kalakaua Ave., tel. 808/923–7927); nine at the **Diamond Head Tennis Center** (3098 Paki Ave., tel. 808/923–7927); and 10 at **Ala Moana Park** (tel. 808/521–7664). Several Waikiki hotels have tennis facilities open to nonguests, but guests have first priority. The **Ilikai Waikiki Hotel** (1777 Ala Moana Blvd., tel. 808/949–3811) has seven courts, one lighted for night play, plus a pro shop, daily tennis clinics, instruction, a ball machine, and a video. The hotel also offers special tennis packages that include room and court fees. There's one court at the **Hawaiian Regent Hotel** (2552 Kalakaua Ave., tel. 808/922–6611), with lessons and clinics by Peter Burwash International. The two courts at the **Pacific Beach Hotel** (2490 Kalakaua Ave., tel. 808/922–1233) also offer instruction.

Water Sports

The seemingly endless ocean options can be arranged through any hotel travel desk or beach concession or at the **Waikiki Beach Center,** next to the Sheraton Moana Surfrider.

Deep-Sea Fishing For fun on the high seas, try **Coreene-C Sport Fishing Charters** (tel. 808/536–7472), **Island Charters** (tel. 808/536–1555), or **Tradewind Charters** (tel. 808/533–0220). Another reliable outfit is **ELO–1 Sport Fishing** (tel. 808/947–5208). All are berthed in Honolulu's Kewalo Basin. Plan to spend $85–$110 per person to share a boat for a full day (7 AM–3:30 PM). Half-day rates are $50–$65. Boat charters run $425–$595 for a full day and $325–$495 for a half day. All fishing gear is included, but lunch is not. The captain usually expects to keep the fish. Tipping is customary, and $20 to the captain is not excessive, especially if you keep the fish you caught.

Sailing Lessons may be arranged through **Tradewind Charters** (350 Ward Ave., Honolulu 96814, tel. 808/533–0220). Instruction follows American Sailing Association standards. Cost: $35 per hour for the first student, $15 for each additional student, up to four. Transportation from Waikiki is available. Tradewinds specializes in intimate three-hour sunset sails for a maximum of six people at $59 per person, including hors d'oeuvres, champagne, and other beverages. The same price will buy you a half-day snorkel or scuba sail.

Silver Cloud Limousine Service (Box 15773, Honolulu 96830, tel. 808/524–7999) arranges private yacht charters, complete with limousine pickup at your hotel. A four-hour sail for one to six passengers is $450, and a seven-hour sail is $550.

Scuba Diving and Snorkeling **South Seas Aquatics** (2155 Kalakaua Ave., Suite 112, Honolulu 96815, tel. 808/735–0437 or 800/252–6244) offers a beginning scuba course for $65 and a two-tank boat dive for $70.

The most famous snorkeling spot in Hawaii is Hanauma Bay (*see* Chapter 4). **Seahorse Snorkeling** (6650 Hawaii Kai Dr., Suite 109, Honolulu 96825, tel. 808/395–8947) has a half-day Hanauma Bay excursion for $5.99, including transportation and equipment. **Steve's Diving Adventures** (1860 Ala Moana Blvd., Honolulu 96815, tel. 808/947–8900) offers the same for $7.

Ocean Kayaking This relatively new sport to the islands is catching on fast. You sit on top of a one-person board and paddle on both sides— great fun for catching waves or just exploring the coastline. Bob Twogood, a name that is synonymous with Oahu kayaking, runs a shop called **Twogood Kayaks Hawaii** (46–020 Alaloa St., Suite B-6, Kaneohe, tel. 808/262–5656), which makes and sells the fiberglass craft and runs free demonstrations on Kailua Beach at least every two weeks. Twogood rents kayaks for $20 a half day, $25 a day, and $40 a weekend.

Surfing If you'd like to look into free surfing lessons, call the **Honolulu Department of Parks and Recreation** (tel. 808/527–6343) to see if it has a clinic scheduled.

Windsurfing This sport was born in Hawaii, and Oahu's Kailua Beach is its cradle. World champion Robby Naish and his family build and sell boards, rent equipment, run "windsurfari" tours, and offer instruction. **Naish Hawaii** (155A Hamakua Dr., Kailua 96734, tel. 800/262–6068). Across the street from Naish is **Windsurfing Hawaii** (156C Hamakua Dr., Kailua 96734, tel. 808/261–3539), another shop with a complete line of boardsailing equipment and accessories as well as rentals. Closer to Kailua Beach's sailing, consider **Kailua Sailboard Company** (130 Kailua Rd., Kailua 96734, tel. 808/262–2555). This shop rents equipment and provides carts to roll it to the waterfront five minutes away.

Spectator Sports

Basketball

Each April, four teams of the nation's best players shoot and dribble during the **Aloha Basketball Classic** at the Neal Blaisdell Center (777 Ward Ave., Honolulu, tel. 808/948–7523).

Football

The **Pro Bowl,** featuring the NFL elite, is played here a week after the Super Bowl. In December collegiate football hits the stadium during the **Aloha Bowl.** The **Hula Bowl,** held each January at Aloha Stadium in Honolulu (tel. 808/486–9300), is a sports classic bringing together All-American college stars and presenting a field full of hula girls at halftime. For local action, the **University of Hawaii Rainbows** take to the field at Aloha Stadium in season, with a big local following. There are often express buses from Kapiolani Park (tel. 808/531–1611 for details).

Golf

The giants of the greens return to Hawaii every January or February (depending on television scheduling) to compete in the **Hawaiian Open Golf Tournament,** a PGA tour regular with a $1 million purse. It is held at the exclusive Waialae Country Club (4997 Kahaha Ave., tel. 808/734–2151) near Waikiki, and it's always mobbed.

Polo

Mokuleia on the North Shore is a picturesque oceanside setting for weekly polo matches. Local teams compete against international players during the season, which runs from March to August. *Dillingham Field, tel. 808/637–POLO. Admission: $5 adults and children 12–17. Food concession available, or pack a tailgate picnic. Game: 2 PM.*

Rugby

Every other year in October, the **Pan Am World International Rugby Tournament** takes place at Kapiolani Park.

Running

The Honolulu Marathon is a thrilling event to watch as well as to participate in. Join the throngs who cheer at the finish line at Kapiolani Park as internationally famous and local runners tackle the 26.2-mile challenge. It's held on a Sunday in December and is sponsored by the Honolulu Marathon Association (tel. 808/734–7200).

Surfing

For two weekends each March, **Buffalo's Annual Big-Board Surfing Classic** fills Makaha Beach with Hawaiian entertainment, food booths, and the best in big-board surfing (tel. 808/696–3878 or consult the newspaper). In the winter you can head out to the north shore and watch the best surfers in the world hang ten during the **Triple Crown Hawaiian Pro Surfing Championships.** This two-day event, scheduled according to the wave conditions, is generally held at the Banzai Pipeline and Sunset Beach during November and December. Watch the newspapers for details.

Volleyball

This is an extremely popular sport in the Islands, and no wonder. The **University of Hawaii Rainbow Wahines** (women's team) has blasted to a number-one league ranking in years past. Crowded, noisy, crazy, and very exciting home games are played during the September–December season in Klum Gym (1337 Lower Campus Rd., Honolulu, tel. 808/948–6376). Admission: $4.

Windsurfing

Watch the pros as they jump and spin on the waves during July's **Pan Am Hawaiian Windsurfing World Cup** off Kailua Beach. There are also windsurfing competitions off Diamond Head point; consult the sports section of the daily newspaper for details on these events.

7 Dining

The strength of Hawaii's tourist industry has allowed Oahu's hotels to attract and pay for some of the best culinary talent in the world. Consequently, Honolulu is one of the few cities where the best dining in town is in the hotels, and Waikiki is the area where you will pay the highest dinner prices.

A wide variety of restaurants serve excellent ethnic food, especially Chinese and Japanese. So pervasive is the Eastern influence that even the McDonald's menu is posted in both English and *kanji*, the universal script of the Orient. In addition to its regular fare, McDonald's serves saimin, a Japanese noodle soup that ranks as the local favorite snack.

Honolulu is most, but not all, of the Oahu dining picture. As you head away from town there are a handful of culinary gems sparkling among many lesser restaurants not worth a second look. So diverse are the island's restaurants that on successive nights you may eat with silver and fine linen napkins, from monkey-pod dishes, with chopsticks, or with your fingers. There may be candlelight, moonlight, or neon light. You can choose from some of the most delectable fish, including *opakapaka* (blue snapper) and mahimahi (white dolphin fish, not to be confused with Flipper). Or you may want to tackle a bowl of brown paste called poi, the traditional starch that Hawaiians lap up with love.

For snacks and fast food around the island, look for the *manapua* wagons, the food trucks usually parked at the beaches; and *okazu-ya* stores, the local version of delis, which dispense tempura, sushi, and plate lunch, Hawaii's unofficial state dish. A standard plate lunch has macaroni salad, "two scoops rice," and an entrée that might be curry stew, kalua (roasted) pig and cabbage, or sweet-and-sour spareribs.

New dining spots keep opening their doors at Restaurant Row (500 Ala Moana Blvd., tel. 808/538–1441) in downtown Honolulu. For a mere 50¢, there's a trolley service between Waikiki and Restaurant Row Thursday–Sunday 5:30–9:15 PM. A free shuttle service is also available between Honolulu's business district and Restaurant Row on weekdays 11:20 AM–1 PM.

Few restaurants require men to wear jackets. An aloha shirt and pants for men and a simple dress or pants for women are acceptable in all but the fanciest establishments. Restaurants are open daily, unless otherwise noted.

The following credit card abbreviations are used: AE, American Express; DC, Diners Club; MC, MasterCard; and V, Visa.

Highly recommended restaurants in each area are indicated by a star ★.

Category	Cost*
Very Expensive	over $60
Expensive	$40–$60
Moderate	$20–$40
Inexpensive	under $20

per person excluding drinks, service, and sales tax (4%)

Waikiki

American
★ **Orchids.** You can't beat the setting, right beside the sea, with Diamond Head looming in the distance and fresh orchids everywhere. The restaurant is terraced, so every table inside and out has a view. The popovers are huge, and the salads are light and unusual. The most popular meal of the week here is the special Sunday brunch, featuring table after table of all-you-can-eat buffet delights; one spread features an impressive variety of Island sashimi. Chafing dishes give you a range of options, from eggs Benedict to chicken curry. Desserts, such as plum cake, are all made in the Halekulani's own kitchen. *Halekulani Hotel, 2199 Kalia Rd., tel. 808/923-2311. Reservations advised. Dress: casual. AE, DC, MC, V. Moderate.*

Eggs 'N Things. This breakfast-only eatery with unusual hours is popular in part for its waitresses. They have names like Mitch and Yoshi, and their breezy, chatty style makes you feel right at home. Late-night revelers often stop here after a night on the town. Omelets are as huge as your plate and come with a variety of fillings; chili and cheese is a favorite. Blackened Cajun-style fish is great with scrambled eggs, and the macadamia nut waffle topped with whipped cream is rich enough to be called dessert. The best bargain is the $1.99 Early Riser Special, two eggs and three pancakes, served 5–9 AM, 1–2 PM, and 1–2 AM. *1911 Kalakaua Ave., tel. 808/949–0820. No reservations. Dress: casual. No credit cards. Open 11 PM–2 PM. Inexpensive.*

Harry's Cafe and Bar. Located right in the thick of the action at the Hyatt Regency Waikiki, this sidewalk cafe in an atrium with a waterfall is a great place to take in the passing parade of people. The reasonably priced menu includes no entrées but does boast some tasty sandwiches, homemade croissants, and other deli treats. The California salad features marinated shrimp, avocado, and tons of fresh vegetables. Another winner is the salmon with bagel chips and cream cheese. *Hyatt Regency Waikiki Hotel, 2424 Kalakaua Ave., tel. 808/922–9292. Dress: casual. AE, DC, MC, V. Inexpensive.*

Hau Tree Lanai. Renovations have made this restaurant right beside the sand at Kaimana Beach more charming than ever. It is often overlooked and shouldn't be. At breakfast, lunch, or dinner, you can dine under graceful hau trees and hear the whisper of the waves. Breakfast offerings include a huge helping of eggs Benedict, a fluffy Belgian waffle with your choice of toppings (strawberries, bananas, or macadamia nuts), and a tasty fresh salmon omelet. This is the only restaurant we know of that features an authentic Japanese-style breakfast with a raw egg, fish, rice, miso soup, and other delicacies. *New Otani Kaimana Beach Hotel, 2863 Kalakaua Ave., tel. 808/923–1555. Reservations required at dinner. Dress: casual. AE, DC, MC, V. Inexpensive.*

Wailana Coffee House. If you like coffee shops, this is a reliable one. Nothing fancy—just booths and tables, waitresses who look like someone's favorite auntie, and all the coffee you can drink. Pancakes, waffles, omelets, and everything else that goes with breakfast are among the specialties of this budget diner. *1860 Ala Moana Blvd., tel. 808/955–1764. Dress: casual. AE, DC, MC, V. Inexpensive.*

Chinese
★ **Golden Dragon.** Local Chinese people consider this the best. Chef Dai Hoi Chang has been here for 30 years and has

Waikiki Dining

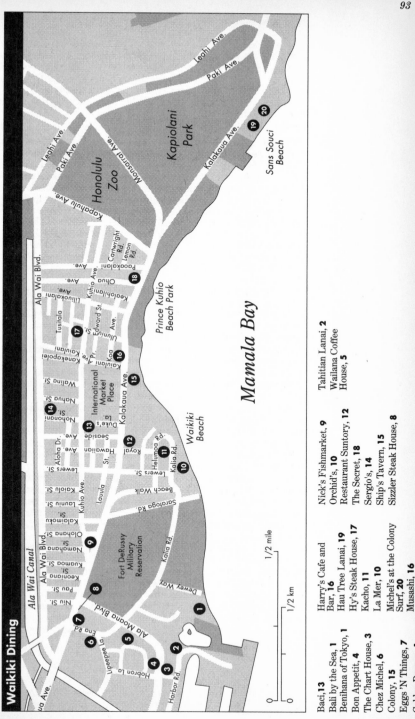

Baci, **13**
Bali by the Sea, **1**
Benihana of Tokyo, **1**
Bon Appetit, **4**
The Chart House, **3**
Chez Michel, **6**
Colony, **15**
Eggs 'N Things, **7**
Golden Dragon, **1**

Harry's Cafe and
Bar, **16**
Hau Tree Lanai, **19**
Hy's Steak House, **17**
Kacho, **11**
La Mer, **10**
Michel's at the Colony
Surf, **20**
Musashi, **16**

Nick's Fishmarket, **9**
Orchid's, **10**
Restaurant Suntory, **12**
The Secret, **18**
Sergio's, **14**
Ship's Tavern, **15**
Sizzler Steak House, **8**

Tahitian Lanai, **2**
Wailana Coffee
House, **5**

developed quite a tasty bill of fare, including Szechuan, Cantonese, and unconventional nouvelle Chinese cuisine. Set right by the water, the restaurant has a stunning red-and-black decor, with big lazy Susans in the middle of each table for easy sharing of food. Among the best items are stir-fried lobster with *haupia* (coconut), and Szechuan beef. The Peking duck and beggar's chicken (whole chicken baked in a clay pot) must be ordered 24 hours in advance. *Hilton Hawaiian Village, 2005 Kalia Rd., tel. 808/949–4321. Reservations required. Dress: casual. AE, DC, MC, V. Moderate.*

Continental
★ **Bali by the Sea.** Like the island it's named for, this restaurant is breeze-swept and pretty, with an oceanside setting offering glorious views of Waikiki Beach. But don't be fooled by the name. This is not an Asian ethnic eatery but an internationally acclaimed restaurant featuring such entrées as roast duck with papaya puree and macadamia nut liqueur. Another favorite is the poached mahimahi and opakapaka, a pair of island fish served with two sauces. Pastry chef Gale O'Malley is the only American pastry chef to have been decorated by the French government. His magnificent tarts, cakes, and sweets are displayed on the rolling pastry cart. *Hilton Hawaiian Village, 2005 Kalia Rd., tel. 808/949–4321. Reservations advised. Dress: casual. AE, DC, MC, V. Expensive.*

★ **Michel's at the Colony Surf.** With mirrors, candlelight, piano music, crystal, and chandeliers, this is easily the most romantic restaurant in town. One wall opens up to panoramas of the sea, lovely by day or night. The service is superb, and the waiters' mastery of tableside cooking is a wonder to behold. For starters, try the lobster bisque, flamed with cognac and laced with lobster chunks and homemade croutons. Pepper steak flamed with Jack Daniels whiskey is another winner. Breakfast, an insider's secret, features crepes suzette sautéed with fruit. *Colony Surf Hotel, 2895 Kalakaua Ave., tel. 808/923–6552. Reservations required. Dress: casual at breakfast, jacket required at dinner. AE, DC, MC, V. Expensive.*

The Secret. Formerly known as The Third Floor, this elegant restaurant feels like Europe—maybe Spain—with extravagant food displays and huge wicker chairs in which to hide. You start off with a yogurt-based nan bread baked in an earthen oven, with pâté, then move on to a wonderful variety of seafoods and other entrees. Complimentary bon-bons served atop a mini-volcano of dry ice follows the five-tiered dessert cart. *Hawaiian Regent Hotel, 2552 Kalakaua Ave., tel. 808/ 922–6611. Reservations required. Dress: casual. AE, DC, MC, V. Expensive.*

Ship's Tavern. The Sheraton Moana Surfrider's signature dining room uses soft spotlights on each table rather than candlelight. The restaurant features French Continental cuisine with a touch of local nouvelle. It also has an array of fresh seafood specialties. *Sheraton Moana Surfrider Hotel, 2353 Kalakaua Ave., tel. 808/922–3111. Reservations advised. Dress: casual. AE, DC, MC, V. Expensive.*

French
★ **La Mer.** In the exotic, elegant atmosphere of a Mandalay mansion, you'll be served a unique blend of French and nouvelle Hawaiian cuisine that most connoisseurs consider the finest dining experience in Hawaii. Portions are delicate and beautifully presented. A favorite appetizer is new-potato salad with sour cream and caviar, and a standout among the entrées is breast of duck with fresh pears and spiced apples in a light gin-

ger sauce. Each evening there are two complete dinner menus, which run $65–$90, soup through dessert. Highly recommended is the cheese and port course, offered in lieu of dessert. *Halekulani Hotel, 2199 Kalia Rd., tel. 808/923–2311. Reservations required. Jacket required. AE, DC, MC, V. Very Expensive.*

Chez Michel. Tinkling fountains, lattice work, and big wicker chairs are the background for prime French cuisine. If you want to impress someone with an insider's touch of class, this is the spot. *Eaton Square, 444 Hobron La., tel. 808/955–7866. Reservations advised. Dress: casual. AE, DC, MC, V. Expensive.*

Bon Appetit. Country French cuisine is presented in a cozy atmosphere reminiscent of a European bistro. Elegantly decorated in pink and black with French-style paintings on the wall, this restaurant is the brainchild of owner-chef Guy Banal, who has created a fascinating menu. Appetizers include a Scandinavian plate of Norwegian salmon and trout marinated in champagne with Gravlak sauce (cream, mustard, horseradish, lemon juice, and dill). Tempting entrées include broiled fresh fillet of fish with ginger-lobster butter, and broiled lamb with sweet pimientos, fresh basil, mint, and garlic. The fixed-price dinner goes for $21.95. *Discovery Bay, 1778 Ala Moana Blvd., tel. 808/942–3837. Reservations required. Dress: casual. AE, DC, MC, V. Closed Sun. Moderate.*

Italian Baci. This is one of Waikiki's great finds. Tucked away in the Waikiki Trade Center, it's a place you might miss unless you know about it. The spacious interior is decorated with a nice blend of modern and traditional, with chrome finishings and cloth napkins. The service is attentive, and the emphasis is on nouvelle Italian cuisine. The star appetizer is charcoaled shrimp with lime, mint, and feta cheese. You have a long list of pastas from which to choose, headlined by the ever-popular lobster ravioli. *Waikiki Trade Center, 2255 Kuhio Ave., tel. 808/924–2533. Reservations advised. Dress: casual. AE, DC, MC, V. Moderate.*

Sergio's. Sergio Battistetti's popular dining room offers a tantalizing taste of Italy smack-dab in the heart of Waikiki. The atmosphere is sophisticated and romantic, with dark-brown booths providing plenty of intimacy. The appetizer menu offers nearly two dozen hot and cold options, including shiitake mushrooms in butter and garlic or spicy calamari (squid) marinara. Among the 16 pasta dishes is the *bugili puttanesca,* whose wide noodles swim in a tomato sauce spiced by anchovies and capers. Other fine entrées include saltimbocco, osso bucco, veal marsala, and Dover sole, pan-fried or broiled. The wine list is extensive and impressive. *445 Nohonani St., tel. 808/926–3388. Reservations advised. Dress: casual. AE, DC, MC, V. Moderate.*

Japanese Kacho. The city of Kyoto is noted for its fine cuisine, and Kacho
★ is an authentic Kyoto-style restaurant. The tempura teishoku is a complete meal with a good sampling of tastes. The sushi, too, is authentic and fresh. *Waikiki Parc Hotel, 2233 Helumoa Rd., tel. 808/921–7272. Reservations advised. Dress: casual. AE, DC, MC, V. Expensive.*

Benihana of Tokyo. These restaurants are as famous for their theatrical knife work at the *teppan* (iron grill) tables as they are for their food. You are seated at a long table with other diners and together you watch as steak, chicken, seafood, and a variety of vegetables are sliced, diced, tossed, and sautéed before your eyes. There's not much variety to the menu, but it's still a lot of fun. Finish off the meal with some green-tea ice cream, a Benihana tradition. *Hilton Hawaiian Village, 2005 Kalia Rd., tel. 808/955–5955. Reservations required. Dress: casual. AE, DC, MC, V. Moderate.*

Restaurant Suntory. This unique restaurant offers Japanese dining at its most elegant. You can choose to eat in four areas: a sushi bar, a *teppanyaki* room (with food prepared on an iron grill), a *shabu shabu room* (thinly-sliced beef boiled in broth), or a private dining room. The waiters and waitresses are stiff and the atmosphere formal, but the food is very good. Beef sashimi and assorted shellfish top the shabu shabu entrées. A complete *teishoku* dinner served teppanyaki-style includes miso soup, vegetable and fish tempura, rice, and dessert. The sushi chef is a wizard to watch as he creates inventive morsels of delicate raw seafood and rice. *Royal Hawaiian Shopping Center, 2233 Kalakaua Ave., tel. 808/922–5511. Reservations advised. Dress: casual. AE, DC, MC, V. Moderate.*

Musashi. It comes in many moods: communal *teppan* tables (with built-in griddles in the center), a sushi bar, and a standard dining area. Discover authentic *kaiseki* cuisine, the gourmet food of Japan, plus many dishes adapted to Western tastes, such as beginner sushi. You'll experience Japanese food without fear. *Hyatt Regency Waikiki, 2424 Kalakaua Ave., tel. 808/923–1234. Reservations advised. Dress: casual. AE, DC, MC, V. Inexpensive.*

Polynesian
★
Tahitian Lanai. Polynesian with a capital P in setting and menu, it's about the only Waikiki restaurant that regularly draws the downtown business crowd at lunch. Try the landmark eggs Benedict. *Waikikian Hotel, 1811 Ala Moana Blvd., tel. 808/946–6541. Reservations required. Dress: casual. AE, DC, MC, V. Moderate.*

Seafood
★
Nick's Fishmarket. Television and film star Tom Selleck spent so much time here that he went into partnership with the owners and opened another Honolulu restaurant, the Black Orchid. His favorite dish at Nick's is the bouillabaisse, but there are many other wonderful offerings to recommend in this dark, candlelit dining room with black booths and elegant table settings. Nick's special salad with spinach cream dressing is special indeed. Unique to Nick's is the Monterey abalone, served with a Ricci sauce containing morsels of tender fish. For dessert, bananas flambé, beautifully prepared tableside, is as dramatic for the eye as for the palate. *Waikiki Gateway Hotel, 2070 Kalakaua Ave., tel. 808/955–6333. Reservations required. Dress: casual. AE, DC, MC, V. Expensive.*

The Chart House. On the second floor overlooking the Ala Wai Yacht Harbor and the sunset, this is a popular cocktail spot. (Salty dogs may want to visit the Yacht Harbor Pub first, just to the right and below the Chart House, where sailors of all sorts gather to quaff a few and swap tales.) The Chart House decor ranges from varnished wood to saltwater aquariums, glass fishing floats to racing sailboat photos. Dinner specialties include Hawaiian lobster and other seafood, as well as steak. The Dungeness crab is remarkable. *Ilikai Waikiki Hotel, Marina Bldg., 1765 Ala Moana Blvd., tel. 808/941–6669. Reservations advised. Dress: casual. AE, DC, MC, V. Moderate.*

Steak **Colony.** As you walk into this hotel restaurant, you're met with a display case showing the iced steak and seafood specialties of the house. Attention to detail pervades the meal, and this place is known by locals to have consistently fine food. Steak and seafood come in a variety of combinations, but be certain to start off with a visit to the soup and salad bar—one of Waikiki's best. Dessert is raised to new heights, both in the elevated serve-yourself dessert bar and in the selection of cakes, pies, and mousses. *Hyatt Regency Waikiki, 2424 Kalakaua Ave., tel. 808/923–1234. Reservations required. Dress: casual. AE, DC, MC, V. Expensive.*

★ **Hy's Steak House.** Things always seem to go well at Hy's, from the steak tartare and oysters Rockefeller right through to the flaming desserts, such as cherries jubilee. The atmosphere is snug and librarylike, and you can watch the chef perform behind glass. Tuxedoed waiters, catering to your every need, make helpful suggestions about the menu. Hy's is famous for its broiled lobster tail, *kiawe*-broiled rack of lamb ("kiawe" is a mesquite-type wood), and glazed New York peppercorn steak. The Caesar salad is excellent, as are the potatoes O'Brien. *Waikiki Park Heights Hotel, 2440 Kuhio Ave., tel. 808/922–5555. Reservations required. Dress: casual. AE, DC, MC, V. Moderate.*

Sizzler Steak House. This neon-and-chrome, low-budget steak and seafood eatery is designed for people who are stopping in for a quick meal. There's generally an all-you-can-eat special, with soup, salad, and hot bread. You walk through a cafeteria-style line to place your order for such items as fried shrimp, steak, and lobster. Breakfast here is pretty good, and the pancakes are substantial. The salad bar is a popular stop. *1945 Kalakaua Ave., tel. 808/955–4069. No reservations. Dress: casual. No credit cards. Inexpensive.*

Honolulu

American **Hala Terrace.** This restaurant has an open-air setting and a healthy lunch menu that stars unusual salads and vegetarian dishes. There is also a full low-calorie menu, with calories listed, along with more substantial offerings, such as a corned beef sandwich on rye with sauerkraut or the excellent homemade lobster ravioli. The Sunset Supper Menu is an excellent buy and includes tropical chicken coated with coconut. The Hala Terrace is the site of the long-running Danny Kaleikini Show, a delightful Polynesian revue performed Monday through Saturday. *Kahala Hilton Hotel, 5000 Kahala Ave., tel. 808/734–2211. Reservations required. Dress: casual. AE, DC, MC, V. Moderate.*

Sunset Grill. The smell of wood smoke greets you as you enter the Sunset Grill, which specializes in *kiawe*-broiled foods ("kiawe" is a mesquite-type wood). The place is supposed to feel unfinished, with the marble bar top and white tablecloths contrasting nicely with the concrete floors. The salad niçoise, big enough for a whole dinner, includes red-top lettuce, beans, tomato, egg, potatoes, and olives, as well as marinated grilled *ahi* (tuna). The trout and scallops, cooked in a wood oven, are both very good. *Restaurant Row, 500 Ala Moana Blvd., tel. 808/521–4409. Reservations advised. Dress: casual. AE, MC, V. Moderate.*

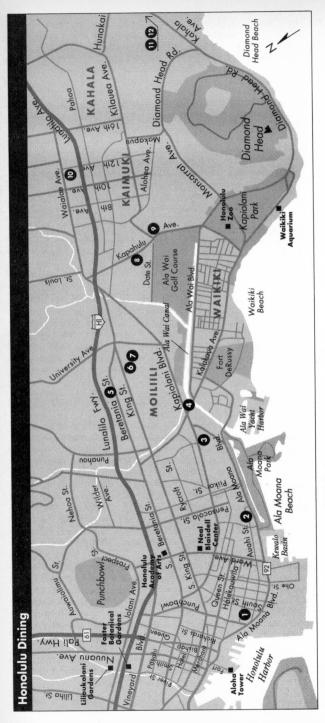

Honolulu Dining

Black Orchid, **1**
Cafe Cambio, **3**
Compadres Mexican
Bar and Grill, **2**
Hala Terrace, **11**
Hard Rock Cafe, **4**

Keo's Thai Cuisine, **9**
Kim Chee Two, **10**
Maile, **11**
Maple Garden, **6**
Ono Hawaiian
Foods, **8**

Philip Paolo's, **5**
Ruth's Chris Steak
House, **1**
Swiss Inn, **12**
The Willows, **7**

★ **The Willows.** Thatched dining pavilions set amid koi, or carp, ponds full of prize fish make this a cherished landmark on Oahu's dining scene. The jungle elegance of the setting makes the perfect backdrop for chef-consultant Kusuma Cooray's golden touch. She has added an international flavor to the tropical entrées, curries, and "mile-high" pies. The sautéed opakapaka with spinach sauce is excellent, as are the lamb medallions in brandy and honey. Hawaiian curry salad is another good choice. For a glimpse of real down-home Hawaii, reserve a space at the Thursdays-only Kamaaina Luncheon. You'll discover lots of local food, music, and spontaneous hula. *901 Hausten St., tel. 808/946–4808. Reservations required. Dress: casual. AE, DC, MC, V. Moderate.*

Hard Rock Cafe. One of the latest links in this international chain of formula restaurants, the Honolulu Hard Rock is filled with musical memorabilia. You can see guitars signed and donated by rock stars, a black outfit once worn by John Lennon, gold and platinum records by the likes of Tina Turner and Michael Jackson, and one of Tom Selleck's aloha shirts. Over the bar hangs a shiny aqua '57 Cadillac woodie. The Hard Rock has mystique but is more famous for its T-shirts than for its food. The menu includes some decent half-pound burgers, ahi (tuna) steak sandwiches, baby back ribs, french fries, and all-American hot apple pie à la mode. Watch out: The oldies can get pretty loud. *1837 Kapiolani Blvd., tel. 808/955–7383. Lunch reservations only. Dress: casual. AE, MC, V. Inexpensive.*

Chinese **Maple Garden.** The fine reputation of Maple Garden is founded on spicy Szechuan cuisine but certainly not on decor. There are some booths, some tables, an oriental screen or two, and lights that are a little too bright at times. It's comfortable, however, and that's all that matters, because the food is delicious. A consistent favorite is the eggplant in a tantalizing hot garlic sauce. *909 Isenberg St., tel. 808/941–6641. Reservations advised. Dress: casual. AE, DC, MC, V. Inexpensive.*

Continental **Black Orchid.** This exceptionally formal restaurant became an immediate success when it opened in 1988, due in part to the fact that Tom Selleck was among its owners. Now it has established itself as a fine dining experience in its own right. Dark wood and the art-deco decor make this a glittering place for lunch or dinner. Black-and-blue ahi (tuna), cooked with Cajun spices, seared on the outside and left raw inside, is reputed to be Selleck's favorite dish, and deservedly so; it is excellent. The best dessert: chocolate mousse with a hazelnut sauce. *Restaurant Row, 500 Ala Moana Blvd., tel. 808/521–3111. Reservations required. Jacket preferred. AE, DC, MC, V. Expensive.*

★ **Maile.** The signature restaurant in this "hotel of the stars" is glamorous and glimmering. Situated on the lower level, the Maile has no view but instead casts an indoor spell with magic all its own. Trickling waterfalls, tropical flowers and greenery, and soft live music create a lovely background to the exceptional dishes, which include both Continental favorites and Island cuisine. Steaks and meats are the pride of the restaurant. Roast duckling Waialae has long been its most famous entrée, prized for its sauce of lychees, bananas, and mandarin orange slices. The gingerbread soufflé laced with cinnamon ice and fresh strawberry compote is a must-try dessert. *Kahala Hilton, 5000 Kahala Ave., tel. 808/734–2211. Reservations required. Jacket advised. AE, DC, MC, V. Expensive.*

Hawaiian **Ono Hawaiian Foods.** Locals frequent this no-frills hangout for a regular hit of their favorite foods. You can tell it's good, because there's usually a line outside after about 5 PM. Housed in a plain storefront site and furnished simply with tables and booths, this small (it seats about 40) restaurant is a good place to do some taste testing of such Island innovations as *poi* (taro paste), *lomilomi* salmon (massaged until tender and served with minced onions and tomatoes), *laulau* (steamed bundle of ti leaves containing pork, butterfish, and taro tops), *kalua* (roasted) pig, and *haupia* (dessert made from coconut). Appropriately enough, the Hawaiian word *ono* means delicious. *726 Kapahulu Ave., tel. 808/737–2275. No reservations. Dress: casual. No credit cards. Inexpensive.*

Italian **Cafe Cambio.** Those in the know love Cafe Cambio for its toned-down trendiness. The unusual decor of this cafe includes imported marble, a mural in pastel shades along one wall, and another wall where you're invited to write your own personal review of the place. Chef-owner Sergio Mitrotti creates every dish himself, cooking what he calls contemporary Northern Italian cuisine. Try the fettuccine al café, made with a hint of fresh-ground espresso coffee in a light-cream Parmesan sauce, and the Italian beer. *1680 Kapiolani Blvd., tel. 808/942–0740. No reservations. Dress: casual. MC, V. Moderate.*

Phillip Paolo's. The talented Phillip Paolo creates Italian cuisine with a flair all his own. The restaurant is set in an old colonial-style house, with rooms of different sizes, wooden floors, and high ceilings. The outdoor garden is a charming place for casual dinners under the trees. The lobster parmigiana is a classic dish, and the steak Capri is served with fresh crab legs and shrimp, all covered with béarnaise sauce. There are always specials here. For dessert, try vanilla cheesecake with a sauce of mangoes from Paolo's own tree. *2312 S. Beretania St., tel. 808/946–1163. Reservations advised. Dress: casual. AE, MC, V. Moderate.*

Korean **Kim Chee Two.** Here's an unassuming little carryout and sit-down restaurant featuring Korean food. The prices are low and the portions are big. You get little side dishes of spicy *kimchee* (pickled vegetables) with your meal. This is a fun place to try such specialties as *bi bim kook soo* (noodles with meat and vegetables), meat *jun* (barbecued beef coated with egg and highly seasoned), *chop chae* (fried vegetables and noodles), and fried *man doo* (plump meat-filled dumplings). *3569 Waialae Ave., tel. 808/737–0006. No reservations. Dress: casual. No credit cards. BYOB. Inexpensive.*

Mexican **Compadres Mexican Bar and Grill.** The after-work crowd gath-
★ ers here for frosty pitchers of potent margaritas and yummy *pupus* (hors d'oeuvres). An outdoor terrace with patio-style furnishings is best for cocktails and chips. Inside, the wooden floors, colorful photographs, and lively paintings create a festive setting for imaginative Mexican specialties. Fajitas, chile rellenos, baby back ribs, and grilled shrimp are just a few of the many offerings. *The Ward Centre, 1200 Ala Moana Blvd., tel. 808/523–1307. No reservations. Dress: casual. AE, MC, V. Inexpensive.*

Steak **Ruth's Chris Steak House.** At last, a steak joint that doesn't look like one, with its pastel-hued and sophisticated decor. Salads are generous, and steak cuts are hefty. The charbroiled fish serves as an excellent alternative to the meat dishes. *Restaurant Row, 500 Ala Moana Ave., tel. 808/599–3860. Reservations recommended. Dress: casual. AE, MC, V. Moderate.*

Swiss   **Swiss Inn.** Waitresses in dirndls and color photos of Alpine vil-
★   lages create a Swiss setting for the concoctions of Swiss-born chef Martin Wyss. Appetizers include *bundnerfleisch* (thinly sliced air-dried beef) and *croûte emmental* (creamed mushrooms on toast with ham and Swiss cheese). Dinners come complete with soup, salad, vegetables, and coffee or tea. Veal medallions Florentine, served on a bed of spinach and covered with sliced bacon and Swiss cheese, is an outstanding entree. With her sparkling aloha spirit, Martin's wife, Jeanie, does an excellent job of keeping things running smoothly. *Niu Valley Shopping Center, 5730 Kalanianaole Hwy., tel. 808/377–5447. Reservations advised. Dress: casual. AE, DC, MC, V. Moderate.*

Thai   **Keo's Thai Cuisine.** Hollywood celebrities have discovered this
★   twinkling nook with tables set amid lighted trees, big paper umbrellas, and sprays of orchids everywhere. In fact, Keo has a whole wall devoted to photos of himself with a variety of stars. The food is exceptional. Favorites include Evil Jungle Prince (shrimp, vegetables, or chicken in a sauce flavored with fresh basil, coconut milk, and red chile) and *chiang mai* salad (chicken salad seasoned with lemongrass, red chile, mint, and fish sauce). Ask for the mild or medium; they'll still be hot, but not as hot as they could be. The crispy Thai noodles have a wonderful, barely-there sauce. The food comes in serving dishes Chinese-style, so you can share. For dessert, the apple-bananas in coconut milk are wonderful, as is the Thai tea with a twist of lemon. *625 Kapahulu Ave., tel. 808/737–8240. Reservations required. Dress: casual. AE, DC, MC, V. Moderate.*

Around the Island

Haleiwa   **Steamer's.** Whether you're seated at a comfortable booth or a
Seafood   table, you'll have the finest meal available on the north shore amid this restaurant's mirrored walls and ceiling fans. The emphasis is on seafood, including a chowder with fresh fish chunks. The meat entrées are not as successful. *Haleiwa Shopping Plaza, 66-165 Kamehameha Hwy., tel. 808/637–5071. Reservations advised. Dress: casual. AE, MC, V. Moderate.*

Hawaii Kai   **Roy's.** Roy Yamaguchi, the widely acclaimed chef of 385 North
Mixed Menu   fame in Los Angeles, has brought his talents to Oahu. His Is-
★   land venture is a two-story restaurant with Pacific colors and casual furnishings. Two walls of windows offer views of Maunalua Bay and Diamond Head in the distance, and a glassed-in kitchen affords equally fascinating views of what's cooking. Roy's cuisine combines the best of Island flavors with French, Italian, Japanese, Thai, and Chinese accents. *Hawaii Kai Corporate Plaza, 6600 Kalanianaole Hwy., tel. 808/396–7697. Reservations advised. Dress: casual. AE, DC, MC, V. Moderate.*

Kaaawa   **Crouching Lion Inn.** This historic residence on the windward
American   side has been a landmark restaurant since 1957. The oceanside setting is dramatic and you have the choice of indoor or outdoor seating. The food is decent enough, with homestyle soups, steaks, seafood, and salads. Specialty of the house is Slavonic

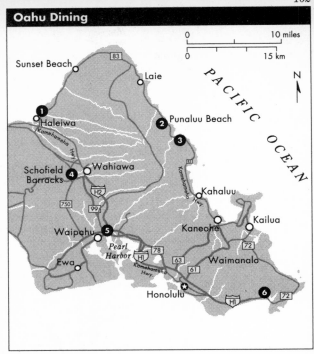

Oahu Dining

steak. *51-666 Kamehameha Hwy., tel. 808/237–8511. Reservations required. Dress: casual. AE, DC, MC, V. Moderate.*

Pearl City
American/Japanese

Pearl City Tavern. Be forewarned: This is a real local hangout. Established in 1944, it boasts the world-famous Monkey Bar, with *live* monkeys who frolic behind glass panels, plus a bonsai garden upstairs and Japanese decorations everywhere. Japanese and American dinners are the fare, including very good beef sukiyaki, ahi (tuna) sashimi and *tonkatsu* (pork cutlet served over rice). *905 Kamehameha Hwy., tel. 808/455–1045. No reservations. Dress: casual. AE, DC, MC, V. Inexpensive.*

Punaluu
Tex/Mex
★

Texas Paniolo Cafe. Saddle up for some countrified fun at this rustic windward retreat. The decor is distinctly south-of-the-border, and the beer is served up in frosty mason jars. Tex-Mex is the food of choice on the enormous menu, which includes jumbo jalapeño burgers, chicken-fried steak, and border-town tacos. *53-146 Kamehameha Hwy., tel. 808/237–8521. No reservations. Dress: casual. AE, MC, V. Inexpensive.*

8 Lodging

Oahu boasts a huge variety of accommodations, so it takes some planning ahead to find your perfect vacation home-away-from-home.

When considering the options, first decide if you want to get away from the everyday hustle and bustle. If your answer is yes, then you should look at the accommodations listed in the "Around the Island" category. If you prefer proximity to the action, go for a hotel or condominium in Honolulu or near Waikiki, where the majority of the island's lodgings are located.

Tiny as it is, Waikiki offers you everything from tidy, simple accommodations (bed, bath, room service, and telephone) away from the beach to elegant oceanside suites furnished with all your heart's desires. There are bed-and-breakfast establishments and condominiums with fully equipped kitchens. If you want a hotel right on the beach in Waikiki, just ask for it. However, Waikiki is small enough that you don't have to pay a premium for a hotel *near* the beach. You can rent a little room three blocks from the ocean and still spend your days on the sand rubbing elbows with the rich and famous.

Some people look at a hotel as simply a place to sleep at night. Others prefer a bit of ambience. The hotels that are recommended in each price category offer a good range of options. A place doesn't have to be expensive to be clean, friendly, and attractive. For a complete list of every hotel and condominium unit on the island, write to the Hawaii Visitors Bureau for the free *Accommodation Guide*. It details amenities and gives each hotel's proximity to the beach.

One asset Oahu's hotels do have in common is the service—in other words, the people with whom you come in contact every day. Their hospitality is part of the aloha spirit, a spirit you can find at the simplest of boarding houses as well as at the top-of-the-line properties. Hawaii's hotel personnel often receive their training at the college level, and tourism is their profession; they have pride in what they do.

Except for the peak months of January, February, and August, you'll have no trouble getting a room if you call ahead of time. When making your reservations, either on your own or through a travel agent, ask about packages and extras. Some hotels have special tennis, golf, or honeymoon deals. Others have periodic room-and-car packages. Oahu hotel prices usually follow a European plan, meaning no meals included.

The following credit card abbreviations are used: AE, American Express; DC, Diners Club; MC, MasterCard; and V, Visa.

Highly recommended hotels in each price category are indicated by a star ★.

Category	Cost*
Very Expensive	over $170
Expensive	$120–$170
Moderate	$75–$120
Inexpensive	under $75

All prices are for a standard double room, excluding 9¼% tax and service charges.

Very Expensive **Halekulani Hotel.** Today's sleek, modern, and luxurious Halekulani was built around the garden lanai and historic 1931 building of the gracious old Halekulani Hotel. Throughout its colorful history, it has attracted visitors looking for an elegant oceanside retreat. The marble-and-wood rooms have accents of white, beige, blue, and gray. All have lanais, sitting areas, refrigerators, bathrobes, and dozens of little touches that are sure to pamper. The in-room check-in service means no waiting in the lobby. The hotel has two of the finest restaurants in Honolulu and an oceanside pool with a giant orchid mosaic. Try to get a room with an ocean view, looking toward Diamond Head. *2199 Kalia Rd., Honolulu 96815, tel. 808/923–2311 or 800/367–2343. On the beach. 456 rooms with bath. Facilities: pool, shops, meeting rooms, 3 restaurants, 3 lounges. AE, DC, MC, V.*

Hawaii Prince Hotel Waikiki. Waikiki's newest hotel is also the final hotel zoned for the heavily developed resort area. On the site of the Old Kaiser Medical Center—adjacent to the well-known "Whaling Wall" mural—the Hawaii Prince opened in April 1990 to enthusiastic reviews. The hotel's architecture and interior design are a departure from the traditional Hawaiian motif, but the businesslike feel of the city hotel works well with views of the nearby Ala Wai Yacht Harbor. Each guest room in the 32-story towers overlooks the boats and the ocean. Every Friday at 5:30 PM yachtsmen raise their sails for a spectacular race out of the channel. Harbor views can be had from the elegant Prince Court restaurant; the Hakone Japanese Restaurant offers dining thrills of another kind. Jazz lovers will find the Captain's Room lounge one of Waikiki's hottest musical venues. *100 Hololmoana St., Honolulu, 96815, tel. 808/956–1111 or 800/ 321–6240. Free beach shuttle for guests. 521 rooms. Facilities: pool, shop, meeting rooms, 4 restaurants, 1 lounge. AE, DC, MC, V.*

★ **Hilton Hawaiian Village.** Hilton spent $100 million to remake this complex into a brand-new, lavishly landscaped resort, the largest in the state. There are four towers, 22 restaurants, three swimming pools, cascading waterfalls, colorful fish and birds, and even a botanical garden of labeled flora. Rooms are decorated in attractive colors of raspberry or aqua, with rattan and bamboo furnishings. The top floor and lower floors of the Rainbow Tower tend to be noisy, but the pricey suites of the Ocean Tower offer all the amenities. A variety of views are offered; ask for an ocean view. The hotel has a private dock for its catamaran and a fine stretch of oceanfront. *2005 Kalia Rd., Honolulu 96815, tel. 808/949–4321 or 800/HILTONS. On the beach, 2,523 rooms with bath. Facilities: 2-tier superpool (10,000 sq. ft.), 2 additional pools, 22 restaurants, 11 lounges. AE, DC, MC, V.*

★ **Hyatt Regency Waikiki.** The focal point of this twin-towered beauty is the 10-story atrium lobby with its two-story waterfall and mammoth metal sculpture. Shops, concerts, and Harry's Bar make this one of the liveliest lobbies anywhere, though you may get lost in it. Each guest room has an oriental art print to complement the warm earth tones, wall-to-wall carpeting, private lanai, color TV, air-conditioning, and combination desk/ game table and chairs. Spats is the hotel's fun Italian restaurant and disco, and Trappers presents hot live jazz. Since the hotel has two towers, there are two Regency Clubs and eight

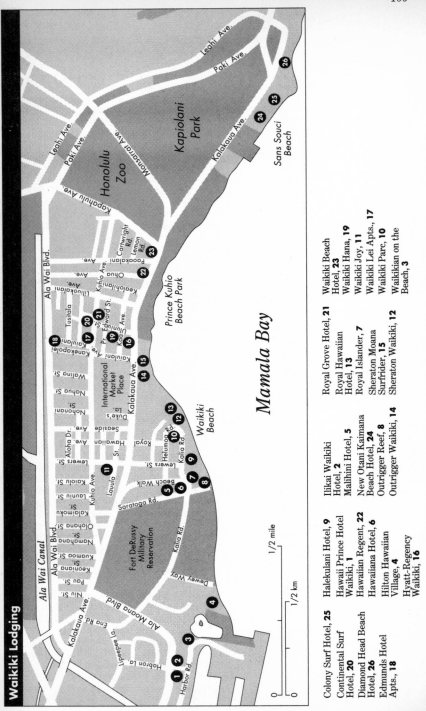

Waikiki Lodging

106

Colony Surf Hotel, **25**
Continental Surf Hotel, **20**
Diamond Head Beach Hotel, **26**
Edmunds Hotel Apts., **18**

Halekulani Hotel, **9**
Hawaii Prince Hotel Waikiki, **1**
Hawaiian Regent, **22**
Hawaiiana Hotel, **6**
Hilton Hawaiian Village, **4**
Hyatt-Regency Waikiki, **16**

Ilikai Waikiki Hotel, **2**
Malihini Hotel, **5**
New Otani Kaimana Beach Hotel, **24**
Outrigger Reef, **8**
Outrigger Waikiki, **14**

Royal Grove Hotel, **21**
Royal Hawaiian Hotel, **13**
Royal Islander, **7**
Sheraton Moana Surfrider, **15**
Sheraton Waikiki, **12**

Waikiki Beach Hotel, **23**
Waikiki Hana, **19**
Waikiki Joy, **11**
Waikiki Lei Apts., **17**
Waikiki Parc, **10**
Waikikian on the Beach, **3**

penthouses. *2424 Kalakaua Ave., Honolulu 96815, tel. 808/ 923–1234 or 800/233–1234. Across the street from the beach and a short walk from Kapiolani Park. 1,230 rooms with bath. Facilities: 7 restaurants; 6 lounges, including a disco and a jazz club; a pool; 70 shops. AE, DC, MC, V.*

★ **Royal Hawaiian Hotel.** This "Pink Palace of the Pacific" was built in 1927, an age of gracious and leisurely travel when people sailed on Matson luxury liners and spent months at the Royal. As befits that grand era, the hotel has high ceilings, period furniture, and flowered wallpaper. People who have been coming here for 30 years insist on a favorite chair or bureau, but the hotel appeals to newlyweds as well as old-timers. Dreams are made of breakfast at the beachside Surf Room, the pink telephones in each room, the corridors of pink carpeting, and the great crystal chandeliers tinkling in the wind. The modern wing is more expensive, but for charm, the original building can't be beat. *2259 Kalakaua Ave., Honolulu 96815, tel. 808/ 923–7311 or 800/325–3535. On the beach. 550 rooms with bath. Facilities: pool, meeting rooms, 2 restaurants, 2 lounges. AE, DC, MC, V.*

★ **Sheraton Moana Surfrider.** The Moana Hotel, the "First Lady of Waikiki," was built in 1901 and restored to her original grandeur in 1989. Sheraton has taken great pains and spent millions on this landmark structure, which has been merged with the newer Surfrider next door. Accommodations retain their cozy charm, and, as in the old days, the furnishings on each floor are made of a different kind of wood: mahogany, oak, maple, cherry, and rare Hawaiian koa. Each room has a colonial-reproduction armoire and such modern amenities as a minibar, in-room movies, Hawaiian soaps and toiletries, a hair dryer, daily newspaper delivery, and 24-hour room service. The Banyan Court is still the focal point for beachside activity, and you can relax on the gracious veranda, sip tea, and tune yourself in to turn-of-the-century living. *2365 Kalakaua Ave., Honolulu 96815, tel. 808/922–3111 or 800/325–3535. On the beach. 803 rooms with bath. Facilities: pool, recreation deck, shops, meeting rooms, 3 restaurants, 3 lounges, poolside snack stand, beach bar. AE, DC, MC, V.*

Expensive **Colony Surf Hotel.** This small hotel with impeccable and
★ personal service is like a condominium; each unit is equipped with a full kitchen and an attractive living area. The same is true of the hotel's annex, the **Colony Surf East,** though units are smaller there. Wealthy patrons like to keep this one a secret; they appreciate the fine points, such as a staff that will hold your aloha shirts and beach paraphernalia until your next visit. The hotel is way up on the Diamond Head (east) end of Waikiki, beyond the mainstream. Its restaurant, Michel's, is French, fashionable, open to the sea, and considered the most romantic dining room in town. *2895 Kalakaua Ave., Honolulu 96815, tel. 808/923–5751 or 800/252–7873. On the beach. Of 171 units, 50 are available for booking. There are an additional 50 units in the Colony Surf East. Facilities: 2 restaurants, 2 cocktail lounges in the 2 buildings. AE, DC, MC, V.*

Diamond Head Beach Hotel. Right on the ocean, but at the quiet end of Waikiki, this is a smaller hotel that appeals to those in search of peaceful accommodations that are still close to the action of Waikiki. Irwin Stroll & Associates, a popular Los Angeles design firm, has decorated many of the rooms with mirrors, glass, and fine fabrics. Some rooms have kitchenettes.

Continental breakfast is served to all guests. *2947 Kalakaua Ave., Honolulu 96815, tel. 808/922–1928 or 800/367–6046. Of 61 units, 53 are available for booking. AE, DC, MC, V.*

Hawaiian Regent Hotel. The huge lobbies and courtyards, open to the breezes, are sunlit and contemporary in feel. With two towers and two lobbies, the layout is a bit confusing, but if you can get past that, this is an outstanding hotel. It has several dining choices, including the award-winning Secret (formerly The Third Floor) and two Japanese restaurants, Regent Marushin and Kobe Fogetsudo. A complimentary breakfast is served each morning, and your bed will be turned down and an orchid left for you each evening. *2552 Kalakaua Ave., Honolulu 96815, tel. 808/922–6611 or 800/367–5370. Across the street from the beach. 1,346 rooms with bath. Facilities: shops, meeting rooms, 2 pools, tennis court, 2 lounges, disco, 6 restaurants. AE, DC, MC, V.*

Ilikai Waikiki Hotel. It's not on the beach, but this is the acknowledged tennis center of Waikiki. It's also one of the closest hotels to the Ala Moana Shopping Center and the popular Ala Moana Beach Park. There are three towers and a huge esplanade, which is always busy, and crowds usually gather for the hula-dancing demonstrations and local musicians. You can get a good look at the Ala Wai Yacht Harbor from here, and Annabelle's lounge atop the hotel affords the best view of Waikiki. *1777 Ala Moana Blvd., Honolulu 96815, tel. 808/949–3811 or 800/367–8434. 800 rooms with bath. Facilities: 2 pools, 7 tennis courts, meeting rooms, shops, 4 restaurants, 2 lounges. AE, DC, MC, V.*

Outrigger Waikiki Hotel. The star beachfront Outrigger property, located right on Kalakaua Avenue, is in the heart of the shopping and dining action, with some of the nicest sands in Waikiki spread out on the other side. Rooms are decorated with a Polynesian motif, and each has a lanai. Some have kitchenettes, for a higher price. For more than twenty years, the main show room has been the home of the sizzling Society of Seven and the group's Las Vegas–style production. *2335 Kalakaua Ave., Honolulu 96815, tel. 808/923–0711 or 800/737–7777. 529 rooms with bath. Facilities: pool, shops, 6 restaurants, 6 lounges. AE, DC, MC, V.*

Sheraton Waikiki. Towering over its neighbors, this hotel has a lobby done in tones of periwinkle and peach, which look much too sedate in a building of such extravagant proportions. Fortunately, the gigantic capiz-shell chandeliers that clatter in the trade winds have survived the renovations. The rooms are spacious, many with a grand view of Diamond Head. The hotel is located just steps away from the multilevel Royal Hawaiian Shopping Center and next to the Royal Hawaiian Hotel. Be sure to take the glass elevator up to the Hanohano Room, an elegant dining room with breathtaking panoramas of the sea and Waikiki. *2255 Kalakaua Ave., Honolulu 96815, tel. 808/ 922–4422 or 800/325–3535. On the beach. 1,900 rooms with bath. Facilities: 2 pools, shops, meeting rooms, 5 restaurants, 3 lounges. AE, DC, MC, V.*

Waikiki Joy. With rooms ranging in price from Moderate to Very Expensive, this 1988 addition to the Waikiki lodging scene has something for everybody. Some rooms have refrigerators, others have full kitchens, and still others have complete wet bars. There are five types of rooms; one tower has all suites, and another has standard hotel rooms. Bed sizes range from double to king and queen, and you can also ask for ocean or partial ocean views. The common denominators: Each room has a lanai, a Jacuzzi, a deluxe stereo system with Bose speakers, and a control panel by the bed. *320 Lewers St., Honolulu 96815, tel. 808/923–2300 or 800/733–5569. 101 rooms with bath. Facilities: pool, sauna, restaurant, lounge. AE, DC, MC, V.*

★ **Waikiki Parc.** Billing itself as offering "affordable luxury," this hotel lives up to that promise in all essentials except the main entrance, which is down a narrow side street, and the location, which is not on the beach. The lobby is light and airy, with mirrors and pastel tones. Guest rooms are done in cool blues and whites, with lots of rattan, plush carpeting, conversation areas, tinted glass lanai doors, and shutters. Each room features a lanai, a refrigerator, central air-conditioning, an electronic in-room safe, and a high-security electronic-card entry system. The hotel has a fine Japanese restaurant called Kacho and the lovely Parc Café. *2233 Helumoa Rd., Honolulu 96815, tel. 808/ 921–7272 or 800/422–0450. 298 rooms with bath. Facilities: pool, recreation deck, 2 restaurants, 2 shops. AE, DC, MC, V.*

Moderate **Hawaiiana Hotel.** One of the cherished old-timers of Waikiki, this hotel has definitely improved with age. The aloha spirit permeates the place. When you arrive you are offered fresh pineapple, and when you leave you get a flower lei. Two- and three-story sections are arranged around a gorgeous tropical garden, and the sands of Fort DeRussy Beach are a short walk away. Open your door, and the gardens and pools are right there. The decor is simple and basic, and rooms come with electronic safes, air-conditioning, phones, and kitchens. Many have lanais as well. Complimentary newspapers, juice, and coffee are offered each morning on the patio. *260 Beach Walk, Honolulu 96815, tel. 808/923–3811 or 800/367–5122. ½ block from the beach. 95 rooms with bath. Facilities: pool, free washers and dryers. AE, MC, V.*

New Otani Kaimana Beach Hotel. Extensive renovations have taken this establishment a long way. The ambience is cheerful and charming and the lobby has happily maintained its unpretentious feel. Polished to a shine, it is open to the trade winds and furnished with big, comfortable chairs and good magazines. Best of all, the hotel is right on the beach at the quiet end of Waikiki, practically at the foot of Diamond Head. Hotel manager Steve Boyle has received national recognition for his efforts to preserve the beauty of Diamond Head, and he often leads hikes to the summit. The staff is also friendly and helpful. Rooms are smallish but very nicely appointed, with soothing pastels, off-white furnishings, and color TV. Get a room with an ocean view, if possible. *2863 Kalakaua Ave., Honolulu 96815, tel. 808/923–1555 or 800/421–8795 in the United States and Canada; in California, 800/252–0197. 125 rooms with bath. Facilities: 3 restaurants (1 Japanese), lounge, shops, meeting rooms. AE, DC, MC, V.*

Outrigger Reef Hotel. The big recommendations here are the location right on the beach and the price—which is right. The extensive renovations have definitely improved the appearance of the lobby and rooms. Charming fashion and souvenir boutiques have replaced the random lobby vendors, and the rooms are now done in soft mauves and pinks; many have lanais, and all have air-conditioning and color TVs. Ask for an ocean view; the other views are decidedly less delightful. The seventh floor is for nonsmokers. *2169 Kalia Rd., Honolulu 96815, tel. 808/923–3111 or 800/737–7777. 883 rooms with bath. Facilities: pool, 4* *restaurants, 5 lounges, nightclub, shops, meeting rooms. AE, DC, MC, V.*

★ **Waikikian on the Beach.** It's one of the few low-rise hotels left, although it does have a newer, air-conditioned Tiki Tower. This hotel is a little gem, perhaps unpolished in spots, but the romance of old Hawaii is definitely here in the South Seas architecture, high-pitched roofs, and jungle-like gardens. Rooms are decorated in old Polynesian style, very different from more modern accommodations, and windows and doors open onto a garden path. The hotel is not technically on the beach, but it fronts the Duke Kahanamoku Lagoon, which has a sandy shore. The Tahitian Lanai restaurant has a faithful local following. *1811 Ala Moana Blvd., Honolulu 96815, tel. 808/949–5331 or 800/922–7866; in Canada, 800/445–6633. 135 rooms with bath. Facilities: pool, shops, restaurant, cocktail lounge. AE, DC, MC, V.*

Waikiki Beach Hotel. The location—almost next to Kapiolani Park, the zoo, and other attractions—is excellent, and the seawall in front of the hotel offers the best sunset views. The mauka (north) tower has been completely refurbished and offers mainly ocean views. The rooms have nice rattan furniture, right down to the headboards. Each room is equipped with a color TV, private lanai, and air-conditioning. The Captain's Table serves meals in surroundings modeled after old-time luxury liners. *2570 Kalakaua Ave., Honolulu 96815, tel. 808/922–2511 or 800/877–7666. Across the street from the beach. 716 rooms with bath. Facilities: pool, 2 restaurants, 3 lounges, shops. AE, DC, MC, V.*

Waikiki Hana. Behind the Hyatt Regency sits this little-known secret, a moderately priced hotel in a superb location. Although the building is not new, it has been renovated, and the lobby is charmingly furnished with wicker furniture. The rooms are attractively decorated, with pink walls, blue quilted bedspreads, and light wood. Each room has a color TV, a telephone, and air-conditioning. Some have kitchenettes. All that, and it's just a block to the beach (the hotel has no pool). Go during the off-season, and the prices are $10 lower. *2424 Koa Ave., Honolulu 96815, tel. 808/926–8841 or 800/367–5004. 73 rooms with bath. AE, DC, MC, V.*

Inexpensive **Continental Surf Hotel.** One of the great budget hotels of Waikiki, this appealing high rise is located along the Kuhio Avenue strip, two blocks from the ocean and convenient to tons of shopping and dining options. The lobby is large and breezy, and the comfortable rooms are decorated in standard Polynesian hues of browns and golds. Each room has a color TV, a telephone, and air-conditioning. However, the units have limited views and no lanais. Some rooms have a well-equipped kitchenette. *2426 Kuhio Ave., Honolulu 96815, tel. 808/922–2755 or 800/ 245–7873. 2 blocks from the beach. 140 rooms with bath. Facilities: guests may use the facilities of its sister hotel, the Miramar, 1½ blocks away. AE, DC, MC, V.*

Edmunds Hotel Apartments. Located on the Ala Wai Canal, four blocks from the ocean, this has been a budget gem for more than 20 years. Long lanais wrap around the building so that each room has its own view of the pretty canal and glorious Manoa Valley beyond—views that look especially lovely at night, when lights are twinkling up the mountain ridges. The rooms are small, nondescript studios, but they have all the basics: kitchenette, toaster, ironing board, and TV set. If you can put up with the occasional sounds of traffic on the boulevard, this is a real bargain. *2411 Ala Wai Blvd., Honolulu 96815, tel. 808/923–8381. 4 blocks from the beach. 12 rooms with bath. No credit cards.*

Malihini Hotel. There's no pool, it's not on the beach, none of the units has a television or air-conditioning, and the rooms are spartan. Still, the atmosphere of this low-rise complex is cool and pleasant, and the gardens are well maintained. All rooms are either studios or one-bedrooms, and all have kitchenettes, daily maid service, and fans. The low prices and good location make this a popular place, so be sure to book well in advance. *217 Saratoga Rd., Honolulu 96815, tel. 808/923–9644. 28 rooms with bath. Facilities: 1 shop. No credit cards.*

Royal Grove Hotel. You won't go wrong with this flamingo-pink hotel, reminiscent of Miami. With just six floors, it is one of Waikiki's smaller hotels. The lobby is comfortable; the rooms, though agreeably furnished, have no real theme and no views. They do, however, all have kitchens and air-conditioning, plus color TVs and telephones. The pool area is bright with tropical flowers (the hotel is not on the beach). Most people enjoy the family atmosphere. *15 Uluniu Ave., Honolulu 96815, tel. 808/ 923–7691. 87 rooms with bath. Facilities: pool. AE, DC, MC, V.*

Royal Islander. The location—only two minutes from a very nice section of Waikiki Beach—is the key to this inexpensive link in the Outrigger hotel chain. The rooms have tapa-print bedspreads and ceramic lamps with matching patterns, and there are Island-inspired pictures on the walls. Each room also has a private lanai, color TV, and air-conditioning. Choose from studios, one-bedroom apartments, or suites. The staff is helpful in arranging activities, such as golf and scuba packages and sightseeing tours. *2164 Kalia Rd., Honolulu 96815, tel. 808/922–1961 or 800/737–7777. 101 rooms with bath. Facilities: no pool, but use of pools at other Outrigger Hotels. AE, DC, MC, V.*

Waikiki Lei Apartments. A favorite with repeat guests looking for affordable lodging in the heart of the action, this four-story pink establishment is one-of-a-kind. There's no elevator; guests use the outside staircase. Everything is well maintained, and the studio units have a kitchen and refrigerator. You need to ask ahead if you want a room with a TV and air-conditioning, and there is no maid service. The decor is dark wood and light-colored spreads, with tile floors. The longer you stay, the lower the daily price. *241 Kaiulani Ave., Honolulu 96815, tel. 808/923–6656 or 808/734–8588. 2 blocks from the beach. 19 units with bath. Facilities: pool, coin-operated washers and dryers. No credit cards.*

Honolulu

Very Expensive
★

Kahala Hilton. Minutes away from Waikiki, on the quiet side of Diamond Head, this elegant and understated hotel is situated in the wealthy neighborhood of Kahala. Here's where kings, Hollywood stars, and presidents stay. The Kahala Hilton's impressive lobby features chandeliers, tropical flower displays, and a musician playing a grand piano. The very large rooms, decorated in earth and natural tones, have his and her dressing rooms and parquet floors. The hotel also has a porpoise pond and three distinguished restaurants, including Maile, with Continental cuisine, and the Hala Terrace supper club, featuring local star Danny Kaleikini. The staff prides itself on its service. The hotel is affiliated with the Maunalua Bay Club, a fitness center just a short shuttle away. *5000 Kahala Ave., Honolulu 96816, tel. 808/734-2211 or 800/367-2525. On the beach. 309 rooms and suites with bath, plus 60 cottage-style units in the Lagoon Terrace. Facilities: pool, tennis court, shops, meeting rooms, 3 restaurants, 2 lounges. AE, DC, MC, V.*

Expensive **Ala Moana Hotel.** This 20-year-old landmark boasts an excellent location, right next to the popular Ala Moana Shopping Center (they're connected by a pedestrian ramp) and one block from Ala Moana Beach Park. A $30 million renovation has transformed the 36-floor hotel into a gorgeous showcase, and the rooms have been refurbished to include color TVs, air-conditioning, AM/FM radios, electronic-card door locks, and private safes. Each has a lanai for a view of the ocean, the Koolau Mountains, or Diamond Head. Preferred floors with special suites feature complete bar service, a spa, and free newspaper and breakfast delivery each morning. The Mahina Lounge, a sleek lobby bar with a white grand piano, hosts live entertainment. *410 Atkinson Dr., Honolulu 96814, tel. 808/955-4811 or 800/367-6025. 1,174 rooms with bath. Facilities: 5 restaurants, 2 lounges, nightclub, shops, pool, pool bar. AE, DC, MC, V.*

Moderate **Manoa Valley Inn.** Here's an intimate surprise tucked away in Manoa Valley, just 2 miles from Waikiki. Built in 1919, this stately hotel features a complimentary Continental-breakfast buffet on a shady lanai, and fresh tropical fruit and cheese in the afternoon. Rooms are furnished in country-inn style, with antique four-poster beds, marble-topped dressers, patterned wallpaper, and fresh flowers. *2001 Vancouver Dr., Honolulu 96822, 808/947-6019 or 800/634-5115. 8 guest rooms, 4 with private bath; 1 cottage with bath. Facilities: TV and VCR in the reading room. MC, V.*

Pagoda Hotel. Minutes away from the four-level, 50-acre Ala Moana Shopping Center and from Ala Moana Beach Park, the Pagoda has a convenient location, and there's also a free shuttle bus between the hotel and its sister property, the Pacific Beach in Waikiki. That, along with the moderate rates, makes this a good choice if you're simply looking for a place to sleep and to catch a couple of meals. Studio rooms include a full-size refrigerator, a stove, and cooking utensils. No real views are offered here, since the hotel is situated in the middle of a lot of high rises. However, the rooms are all air-conditioned, and each has a color TV. The hotel features Koi, one of Honolulu's most interesting restaurants, notable for its Japanese gardens and waterways filled with colorful carp. *1525 Rycroft St., Honolulu 96814, tel. 808/941-6611 or 800/367-6060. 361 rooms with bath. Facilities: pool, shops, 2 restaurants. AE, DC, MC, V.*

Around the Island

Very Expensive **Turtle Bay Hilton.** The only place to stay for miles and miles along the island's north shore. Though it's not swanky, this oceanside retreat has everything it takes for a relaxing stay away from town. The rooms, in three separate wings, have private lanais and are furnished with basic wicker, brass, pastels, and light woods, with pastel prints on the walls. Many people like the hotel for its golf course and horseback-riding facilities. Others drive out just to enjoy its mammoth Sunday champagne

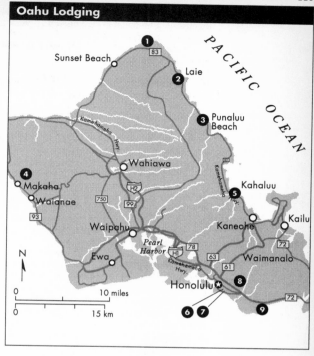

Oahu Lodging

brunch, where you dine next to huge windows with a view of the crashing surf. The sunsets are wonderful, so try to get a room with a view of the water. The cottages adjacent to the hotel are pricier but offer more privacy. *Box 187, Kahuku 96731, tel. 808/293–8811 or 800/HILTONS. On the beach. 486 rooms, suites, and cottages with bath. Facilities: pool, golf, tennis, horses, shops, restaurants. AE, DC, MC, V.*

Expensive   **Sheraton Makaha Resort and Country Club.** It takes an hour-
★ plus by car to get from Waikiki to this country resort set in glorious Makaha Valley, and the trip is worth it. Clusters of low-rise cottages and open-air pavilions keep this place simple and sweet. The Polynesian architecture and steep A-framed roofs look a little dated, but the interiors are done in a lovely combination of natural colors and woods. Each room has a private lanai with chairs and a table, plus a refrigerator, air-conditioning, a telephone, and a color TV. Most of the guests here play golf on one of the two highly acclaimed Makaha courses. Makaha Beach, popular with the locals, is about a mile away. Be sure to sign up for the horseback ride to the valley's restored ancient heiau (sacred Hawaiian site). *Box 896, Makaha 96792, tel. 808/695–9511 or 800/334–8484. 189 rooms with bath. Facilities: golf, tennis, horses, pool, shops, lounge, 2 restaurants. AE, DC, MC, V.*

Inexpensive   **Laniloa Lodge.** Situated on the main road right next to the Polynesian Cultural Center, this plain, two-story establishment is the only hotel in Laie. That means you can break your round-the-island driving tour in two and spend the night here in basic comfort. The rooms are all studios, with color TVs and air-conditioning. The motif is Polynesian. Five separate wings form a circle around the swimming pool, and all the lanais face inward. *55109 Laniloa St., Laie 96762, tel. 808/293-9282 or 800/ LANILOA. 46 rooms with bath. Facilities: pool. AE, DC, MC, V.*

Pat's at Punaluu. Families find everything they need at this unpretentious condominium hotel located between the windward side and the North Shore, an ideal base for seeing the attractions of Oahu's "other side." The mood is decidedly country here. The hotel is set on a reef-protected, palm-fringed beach whose waters are nice for swimming, snorkeling, windsurfing, and fishing. Golf and tennis are also nearby. Fully furnished rental apartments include studio and cottage units with kitchens and dishwashers; many have washer/dryers. Rooms are done in greens and browns, with rattan furniture, and each unit has a lanai. *Box 359, Hauula 96717, tel. 808/293-8111 or 293-9322. On the beach. 136 rooms with bath. Facilities: pool, restaurant, saunas, gym, stores, recreational areas. MC, V.*

Schrader's Windward Marine Resort. Here is another rural resort with fewer luxuries than you would find in Waikiki but with perhaps a little more personalized attention from the staff. Some of the one-, two-, and three-bedroom apartments have kitchens and refrigerators. Each unit has a color TV, air-conditioning, a couch and coffee table; beds are turned down for the guests at night. The fancier rooms include full cooking facilities and remote-control TV. Some rooms open onto Kaneohe Bay, so close that people have been known to fish right off their lanais. Other rooms face the Koolau Mountains. Set on a peninsula, this is a popular spot for water activities. Jet skiing, snorkeling, windsurfing, and other excursions are offered to guests at special rates. *47-039 Lihikai Dr., Kaneohe 96744, tel. 808/ 239-5711 or 800/735-5711. On the beach. 55 rooms with bath. Facilities: water sports, pool, spa. AE, DC, MC, V.*

Bed-and-Breakfasts

Bed and Breakfast Hawaii. This reliable booker offers homestays around Oahu, as well as on the other Islands. *Box 449, Kapaa 96746, tel. 808/822-7771 or 800/733-1632.*

Bed and Breakfast Honolulu. This company has an especially good selection of rooms in Honolulu, including a place to stay in one of the few remaining private homes in Waikiki. *3242 Kaohinani Dr., Honolulu 96817, tel. 808/595-7533 or 800/288-4666.*

Pacific Hawaii Bed and Breakfast. These folks will help you book a B & B unit in the moderate range. *19 Kai Nani Pl., Kailua 96743, tel. 808/262-6026 or 254-5030.*

9 The Arts and Nightlife

The Arts

The arts thrive right alongside the tourist industry in Oahu's balmy climate. The island has a symphony orchestra, an opera company, chamber-music groups, and theater troupes. The major ballet companies also come gliding through from time to time. Check the local newspapers, the morning *Honolulu Advertiser* and the afternoon *Honolulu Star-Bulletin*, for the latest happenings.

Dance

Every autumn, the Honolulu Symphony (tel. 808/537–6191) imports the **San Francisco Ballet.** A local company, **Ballet Hawaii** (tel. 808/988–7578), is active during the holiday season with its annual production of **The Nutcracker,** which is usually held at the Mamiya Theater (3142 Waialae Ave., Chaminade University, Honolulu).

Film

Art films. Art, international, classic, and silent films are screened at the little theater at the Honolulu Academy of Arts. *900 S. Beretania St., Honolulu 96814, tel. 808/538–1006. Tickets: $3. Dinner in the garden courtyard (tel. 808/531–8865) is served Thurs. at 6:30 PM.*

The Hawaii International Film Festival (1777 East–West Rd., Honolulu 96822, tel. 808/944–7666) may not be Cannes, but it is unique and exciting. The week-long festival, held from the end of November to early December, is based on the theme "When Strangers Meet." Top films from the United States, Asia, and the Pacific are aired day and night at several theaters on Oahu. Many local people plan their vacations around this time and spend days viewing free films and attending lectures, workshops, and social events with visiting film experts.

The Varsity Theater (1106 University Ave., tel. 808/946–4144) is a two-theater art house that brings internationally acclaimed motion pictures to Honolulu.

Waikiki generally gets the first-run films at its trio of theaters dubbed, appropriately, the **Waikiki 1, Waikiki 2,** and **Waikiki 3** (tel. 808/923–2394). Check newspapers for what's playing.

Music

Chamber Music Hawaii (tel. 808/261–4290) gives 25 concerts a year at the Honolulu Lutheran Church (1730 Punahou St.), Honolulu Academy of Arts (900 S. Beretania St.), and other locations around the island.

The Hawaii Opera Theater's season spans February and March, and includes such works as Verdi's *Aida*, Mozart's *The Marriage of Figaro*, and Bernstein's *Candide. Neal Blaisdell Concert Hall, Ward Ave. and King St., tel. 808/521–6537. Tickets: $15–$40 at the box office. To charge on credit cards, tel. 808/521–2911. MC, V.*

The Honolulu Symphony's season runs September to April, Tuesday evenings and Sunday afternoons at Blaisdell Concert Hall (Ward Ave. at King St.). The Symphony on the Light Side series is on Friday evenings during the same season. Well-known Island musicians often play with the symphony, and occasionally international performers are headlined. During the summer, the popular Starlight Series is held outdoors at the Waikiki Shell in Kapiolani Park. Write or call for a complete schedule. *1441 Kapiolani Blvd., Suite 1515, Honolulu 96814, tel. 808/942–2200. Tickets: $10–$30.*

During the school year, the faculty of the **University of Hawaii Music Department** (tel. 808/948–7756) gives concerts at Orvis Auditorium on the Manoa campus.

Rock concerts are usually performed at the cavernous Neal Blaisdell Center Arena (tel. 808/521–2911). Internationally famous stars also pack them in at Aloha Stadium (tel. 808/486–9300).

Theater

Because the Islands are so expensive to get to and stay on, major touring companies seldom come to Hawaii. As a result, Oahu has developed several excellent local theater troupes, which present first-rate entertainment all year long.

American Theater Company Hawaii, the newest ensemble on the scene, is Hawaii's only full-fledged professional acting company. It features Broadway actors and local professionals and mounts productions in various locations around town. *720 Iwilei Rd., Suite 290, Honolulu 96817, tel. 808/599–5122. Prices vary.*

The **Diamond Head Theater** is in residence five minutes away from Waikiki, right next to Diamond Head. Its repertoire includes a little of everything: musicals, dramas, experimental, contemporary, and classics. *520 Makapuu Ave., Honolulu 96816, tel. 808/734–0274. Tickets: $11.75–$15.75.*

The **Honolulu Theater for Youth** stages delightful productions for children around the Islands from July to May. Write or call for a schedule. *2846 Ualena St., Honolulu 96819, tel. 808/839–9885. Tickets: $6 adults, $4 youth.*

The **John F. Kennedy Theater** at the University of Hawaii's Manoa campus is the setting for eclectic dramatic offerings—everything from musical theater to Kabuki, Noh, and Chinese opera. *1770 East-West Rd., Honolulu 96822, tel. 808/948–7655. Prices vary.*

Kumu Kahua, now in its 21st season, is the only troupe presenting shows and plays written on and about the Islands. It offers five productions a year in Tenney Theatre, on the grounds of St. Andrew's Cathedral. *224 St. Emma Sq., Honolulu 96813, tel. 808/737–4161. Tickets: $6 adults, $5 students and seniors.*

The **Manoa Valley Theater** gives wonderful nonprofessional productions in an intimate theater in Manoa Valley. Its season is September to June. Write or call for a schedule. *2833 E. Manoa Rd., Honolulu 96822, tel. 808/988–6131. Tickets $12–$14.*

The **Starving Artists Theater Company** is the theater-in-residence at Mid-Pacific Institute. Its creative productions draw on both student and community talent. *2445 Kaala St., Honolulu 96822, tel. 808/942–1942. Tickets: $5–$7.*

The **Windward Theater Guild** is now in its 35th year of offering live family entertainment on the windward side of Oahu. Since it has no theater of its own, check the newspapers for location. *Box 624, Kailua 96734, tel. 808/261–4885. Tickets: $8–$10.*

Nightlife

Nightlife on Oahu can be as simple as a barefoot stroll in the sand or as elaborate as a dinner show with all the glittering choreography of a Las Vegas production. You can view the vibrant hues of a Honolulu sunset during a cocktail cruise, or hear the mystifying melodies of ancient chants at a luau on a remote west-shore beach.

Waikiki is where nearly all of Oahu's night action takes place, and what action there is! Kalakaua and Kuhio avenues come to life when the sun goes down and the lights go on. It's fun just to watch the parade of people. Some strollers walk purposefully, knowing they have dinner reservations. Others wander along the strip reading every sign, every posted menu, looking for something to strike their fancy, whether it's the right atmosphere, the right price, or the catchiest tune.

Outside Honolulu, the offerings are slimmer but equally diverse. You can dance the two-step at a waterfront cafe one night and the next night boogie to live bands in a tiny second-story windward bar. The north shore is more conducive to settling back to the music of a slack-key guitar and lilting falsetto voice, while the ranch country of Waimanalo lends itself to country tunes and fiddle playing.

Wafting through the night air of Oahu is the sound of music of every kind—from classical to contemporary. Music has been the language of Hawaii from the beginning, and Oahu has the best selection of any Island. Along with the music of the ancients, there's a new music in the soul of Hawaii. Traditional Hawaiian music has absorbed or fused with rock and disco to create a distinctively Hawaiian contemporary sound. Strong currents of jazz, country, and reggae also run through the local music pool.

Meanwhile, hula dancers wear sequined skirts in Waikiki and authentic ti-leaf skirts at Paradise Cove; they are accompanied by everything from *ipu* drums to electric guitars, mercifully not on the same stage in most cases. The latest high-tech, ultrastereo video discos may also be found on Oahu, but then, so are acoustic ukulele trios.

Bars/Cabarets/Clubs

The drinking age is 21 on Oahu and throughout Hawaii, although many bars admit younger people without serving them alcohol. By law, all establishments that serve alcoholic beverages must close at 2 AM. The only exceptions are those with a cabaret license, which have a 4 AM curfew. These may be billed as discotheques, but they are required to have live music. Most of the places listed below have a cover charge of $2 to $5.

Waikiki **Annabelle's** (Ilikai Waikiki Hotel, 1777 Ala Moana, tel. 808/949–3811). This spot, which offers disco dancing atop the hotel with the Honolulu city lights spread out below, attracts a casual crowd—what might be classified as the "beer bunch." Happy hour nightly 5–9, open until 2 on weekdays, 4 on weekends.

Bavarian Beer Garden (Royal Hawaiian Shopping Ctr., 3rd floor, 2201 Kalakaua Ave., tel. 808/922–6535). You can polka to your heart's content in this old-world atmosphere and quaff some of the world's best brews. Oktoberfest specials are a big deal each fall. Nightly 5–midnight.

Bobby McGee's Conglomeration (2885 Kalakaua Ave., tel. 808/ 922–1282). The club has disco dancing for adults in the 21–30 age group. Nightly 7–2.

Cilly's (1909 Ala Wai Blvd., basement, tel. 808/942–2952). This is another place where the fast-moving younger-adult crowd goes for disco dancing. Evening drink specials come as cheap as 25¢. Nightly 9–4.

Cupid's Lobby Bar (Prince Kuhio Hotel, 2500 Kuhio Ave., tel. 808/922–0811). Singer and pianist Pat Sylva tickles the ivories Mondays through Thursdays, while on Friday he's joined by friends to form the Pat Sylva Hawaiian Trio. Weekends feature guitar player Scott Moulton. Daily 11–11 with live music 6–10.

Esprit (Sheraton Waikiki Hotel, 2255 Kalakaua Ave., tel. 808/ 922–4422). Bernadette and the Sunshine Company play Tuesday through Saturday, and the Love Notes fill the Sunday and Monday slot. Tourists flock here to dance, and so do local men looking for tourist women. Nightly 9–1.

Genesis Nightclub (2888 Waialae Ave., tel. 808/734–3772). After the dinner show there's dancing to live music amid stainless-steel decor. Nightly 11–3:30.

Hawaii Prince Hotel's Captain's Room (100 Holomoana St., tel. 808/956–1111). Hot sounds of the island's most exciting jazz performers fill this new nightspot. Nightly 10–2.

Jazz Cellar (205 Lewers St., tel. 808/923–9952). Live rock every night and 25¢ drinks on Monday make this a popular spot with the young-adult set. Music nightly 9–4. Late-night happy hour 2–4 AM.

Maile Lounge (Kahala Hilton Hotel, 5000 Kahala Ave., tel. 808/ 734–2211). A band called Kit Samson's Sound Advice has kept folks swinging on the small dance floor for more than 15 years, playing everything from contemporary hits to '40s favorites. Mon.–Sat. 8:15–12:45.

Monarch Room (Royal Hawaiian Hotel, 2255 Kalakaua Ave., tel. 808/923–7311). Tea dancing is a tradition at this historic hotel. Dancers spill out onto the grassy area near the ocean to dance to music by the Del Courtney Orchestra with vocalist Jimmy Borges. Sunday 4–8:30.

Moose McGillycuddy's Pub and Cafe (310 Lewers St., tel. 808/ 923–0751). A variety of bands play for the beach-and-beer gang in a casual setting. Nightly 9–1:30.

Nick's Fishmarket (Waikiki Gateway Hotel, 2070 Kalakaua Ave., tel. 808/955–6333). This is probably the most comfortable of the Waikiki dance lounges, with an elegant crowd, inspiring music, and an intimate, dark atmosphere. There's some singles action here. Nightly 9–1:30.

Nicholas Nickolas (Ala Moana Hotel, 410 Atkinson Dr., tel. 808/955–4466). The view is splendid, the music is good, and the crowd dresses well, but the place is a bit on the stuffy side. Dancing Sunday–Thursday nights 9:30–2:15, Friday and Saturday 10–3:15.

Paradise Lounge (Hilton Hawaiian Village, 2005 Kalia Rd., tel. 808/949–4321). It's expensive, which is reflected in the crowd's appearance. A piano player sets the tone for the dancing, nightly 5:30–11. One of Honolulu's top jazz crooners, Jimmy Borges, headlines with the Betty Loo Taylor Trio Friday and Saturday 8–midnight.

Pink Cadillac (478 Ena Rd., tel. 808/942–5282). The hard rock music draws a rowdy crowd. You can dance by yourself or with your partner. Nightly 9–2.

Point After (Hawaiian Regent Hotel, 2552 Kalakaua Ave., tel. 808/922–6611). This club, with video dancing for young adults, is a cut above most. Nightly 7–4.

Rumours (Ala Moana Hotel, 410 Atkinson St., tel. 808/955–4811). The after-work crowd loves this spot, which offers video and disco dancing with all the lights and action. Sun.–Thurs. nights 5–3, Fri. and Sat. nights 5–4. On Big Chill nights, the club plays oldies from the '60s and '70s and serves free pupus, or hors d'oeuvres (call for schedule).

Scruples (Waikiki Market Place, 2310 Kuhio Ave., tel. 808/923–9530). The club features disco dancing to Top 40 tunes, with a young adult, mostly local crowd. Nightly 8–4.

Shore Bird Beach Broiler (Outrigger Reef Hotel, 2169 Kalia Rd., tel. 808/922–2887). This beachfront disco that spills right out to the sand features a large dance floor and 10-foot video screen. Karaoke singalongs are held nightly, 9–2.

Trappers (Hyatt Regency Waikiki, 2424 Kalakaua Ave., tel. 808/923–1234). This is an elegant night spot featuring such popular musicians as the New Orleans Jazz Band and jazz flautist Herbie Mann. Stars stop by to jam when they're in town. Nightly 5–2.

Wave Waikiki (1877 Kalakaua Ave., tel. 808/941–0424). Dance to live rock 'n' roll until 1:30, recorded music after that. It can be a rough scene, but the bands are tops. Nightly 9–4.

Honolulu   **Anna Banana's** (2440 S. Beretania St., tel. 808/946–5190). At this two-story, smoky dive, the live music is fresh, loud, and sometimes experimental. Local favorites the Pagan Babies perform ultra-creative reggae music regularly, but the likes of blues singer Taj Mahal have been known to slip in for a set or two. Open nightly 11:30–2. Live music Wednesday–Sunday, 9–2.

Black Orchid (Restaurant Row, 500 Ala Moana Blvd., tel. 808/521–3111). A very upscale atmosphere pervades this restaurant and club, which is partially owned by Tom Selleck. Azure McCall sings hot jazz weeknights 5:30–9 and Sundays 8:30–1:30. Live dance bands play Tuesday–Saturday nights 10–3:30.

Buzz's Original Steak House (2535 Coyne St., tel. 808/944–9781). The lounge area of this comfortable restaurant is the forum for mellow folk/jazz singers on Friday and Saturday nights 8–11:30. For a real treat, catch old-time song-writer Andy Cummings as he strolls around strumming his ukulele and telling stories about the old days, Sunday nights 6–9.

Jubilee Nightclub (1007 Dillingham Blvd., tel. 808/845–1568). If you can see through the smoke and hear over the noise, this local hangout is a great spot to experience live, authentic Hawaiian music. It's not a fancy place, so don't dress up. Nightly 8–4.

Studebakers (Restaurant Row, 500 Ala Moana Blvd., tel. 808/526–9888). Exhausting "nonstop bop" revives the early rock 'n' roll era with an all-American '50s and '60s look. Free pupus weekdays 4–8. Open Monday–Saturday 11 AM–2 AM, Sunday noon–2 AM. Minimum age: 23.

Around the Island **Pecos River Cafe** (99–016 Kamehameha Hwy., tel. 808/487–
Aiea 7980). Billing itself as Hawaii's premier country and western
nightclub, this easygoing establishment features two live
bands. Keyed Up Country plays Sunday–Tuesday nights, and
Straight Shot takes over Wednesday–Saturday nights, 9–1:20.

Kahuku **Bayview Lounge** (Turtle Bay Hilton, tel. 808/293–8811). A tru-
ly beautiful place to watch the sun set over the north shore water. Regulars the Ohana Trio play contemporary Hawaiian
tunes Thursday nights 6–9.

Kailua **Fast Eddie's** (52 Oneawa St., tel. 808/261–8561). If you want to
boogie, visit this hot spot for live local and national bands playing everything from rock to Top 40 songs. Nightly 8–4. Attention, ladies: The Fast Eddie's Male Revue is a longstanding
tradition not to be missed. Friday and Saturday nights 8:30–
10:30.

Makaha **Lobby Lounge** (Sheraton Makaha Resort and Country Club,
tel. 808/695–9511). If you're staying at this tranquil resort,
stop in the Lobby Lounge for Karaoke Night, when you can try
your hand at performing, Friday–Saturday 8:30–12:30.

Makapuu **The Galley** (Sea Life Park, Makapuu Point, tel. 808/259–7933).
Some of the top names in Island entertainment play at this relaxed restaurant in the popular marine park. Friday nights
8:30–10, with park admission.

Cocktail and Dinner Shows

Some Oahu entertainers have been around for years, and others have just arrived on the scene. Either way, the dinner-show
food is usually acceptable, but certainly not the main event. If
you want to dine on your own and then take in a show, sign up
for a cocktail show. Dinner shows are all in the $35–$45 range,
with the cocktail shows running $17–$25. The prices usually include one cocktail, tax, and gratuity. In all cases, reservations
are required.

Al Harrington (Polynesian Palace, Reef Towers Hotel, 247
Lewers St., tel. 808/923–9861). Dubbed "the South Pacific
Man," Harrington is a tall, handsome singer with a rich voice
and a cast of 16 musicians and dancers to back him up. Sunday
to Friday, first dinner seating at 5, cocktail seating at 5:45 for
show at 6. Second dinner seating at 8, second cocktail seating at
8:45 for show at 9.

Brothers Cazimero (Monarch Room, Royal Hawaiian Hotel,
2259 Kalakaua Ave., tel. 808/923–7311). Robert and Roland
Cazimero put on a class act, complete with their own hula dancers and a splendid blend of traditional and contemporary Hawaiian tunes. The Monarch Room is a lovely oceanside setting.
Dinner show Tuesday to Saturday at 8:30, cocktail show Friday
and Saturday at 10:30.

Charo (Tropics Surf Club, Hilton Hawaiian Village, 2005 Kalia
Rd., tel. 808/949–4321 or 942–7873). Charo has appeared on
Johnny Carson, David Letterman, and Merv Griffin's shows
and has guest starred on countless television programs. This
"coochie-coochie" girl's latest venture is a live act in one of
Waikiki's newest showrooms, located beachside. Latin
rhythms, flamenco dancing, songs of the Islands, and international music add up to a fiery evening with an explosive per-

former. Dinner seating at 6:30; cocktail seating at 7:30 for the show at 8.

Comedy Club (Ilikai Hotel, 1777 Ala Moana Blvd., tel. 808/922–5998). Some of the most outrageous national and local comics take to the stage of this relatively new and increasingly popular establishment. Show times are Tuesday to Thursday nights at 9; Friday at 8 and 10; Saturday at 7, 9, and 11; and Sunday at 9. There's dancing after the show, too.

Danny Kaleikini (Kahala Hilton Hotel, 5000 Kahala Ave., tel. 808/734–2211). This mellow fellow has been serenading guests for more than 20 years with songs, stories, and an occasional tune on the nose flute. Kaleikini's a gentleman, and a very gifted one. He performs an interesting mix of songs from Hawaii and Japan, where he's also a major star. Book early, because there's rarely an empty table. Dinner and cocktail show Monday to Saturday at 9.

Don Ho (The Dome, Hilton Hawaiian Village, 2005 Kalia Rd., tel. 808/949–4321). Waikiki's old pro still packs them in with his glitzy Las Vegas–style Polynesian revue. His memorable show features a huge cast of attractive performers from around the South Pacific, led by the "King of Hawaiian Entertainment" himself. Dinner seating Sunday to Friday at 6:30, cocktail seating at 8 for an 8:30 show.

Flashback (Hula Hut Theater Restaurant, 286 Beach Walk, tel. 808/923–8411). This is one of Waikiki's biggest draws. The movie-star look-alikes really pour on the nostalgia. The Elvis imitator—Jonathan Von Brana—looks pretty close to the real thing. The faux Diana Ross, Supremes, and Tina Turner are also tops. Monday–Saturday dinner seating begins at 8, cocktail seating at 8:30 on a first-come, first-served basis for the show at 9.

Frank DeLima (Peacock Room, Queen Kapiolani Hotel, 150 Kapahulu Ave., tel. 808/922–1941). Local funny man Frank DeLima presides over this comedy forum. He places a heavy accent on the ethnic humor of the Islands, and does some pretty outrageous impressions. By the end of the evening he's poked fun at everyone in the audience—and folks eat it up. A word of caution: Reserve a stage-side table only if you're up for a personal ribbing. Wednesday–Sunday nights, 9:30 and 11.

Polynesian Cultural Center (55–370 Kamehameha Hwy., Laie, tel. 808/293–3333). Easily one of the best shows on the Islands. The actors are students from Brigham Young University's Hawaii campus. The production has soaring moments and an "erupting volcano." Dinner served from 4:30 on for the 7:30 show. During peak seasons (Christmas to March and June to August) there are two shows, at 6 and 7:45.

Sheraton's Spectacular Polynesian Revue (Ainahau Showroom, Sheraton Princess Kaiulani Hotel, 120 Kaiulani Ave., tel. 808/971–5300). From drumbeats of the ancient Hawaiians to Fijian war dances and Samoan slap dances, this show takes audiences on a musical tour of Polynesia. The highlight is a daring Samoan fire knife dancer. Nightly dinner seating at 5:15, cocktail seating at 6. A fashion show and magic presentation begins at 6; the main revue starts at 6:30.

Society of Seven (Outrigger Waikiki Hotel, 2335 Kalakaua Ave., tel. 808/922–6408). This lively, popular septet has great staying power and, after 20 years, continues to put on one of the best shows in Waikiki. They sing, dance, do impersonations, play instruments, and above all, entertain with their contemporary sound. Monday–Saturday nights, 8:30 and 10:30. No 10:30 show on Wednesday.

Dinner Cruises

The fleet of boats gets bigger every year. Most set sail daily from Fisherman's Wharf at Kewalo Basin, just beyond Ala Moana Beach Park, and head along the coast toward Diamond Head. There's usually dinner, dancing, drinks, and a sensational sunset. You'll find it hard to go indoors to dance, because the sea and sky are just too spectacular. Dinner cruises cost approximately $40, except as noted.

Aikane Catamarans (677 Ala Moana Blvd., Honolulu 96813, tel. 808/522-1533). The table seating for dinner is a plus. This is one of the veteran outfits, with catamarans based on an ancient Hawaiian design. Also offered: a package that takes you to the Outrigger Waikiki Hotel after the cruise to spend the rest of the evening with the Society of Seven entertainers. On Fridays there's a rock 'n' roll cruise, 8–10.

Alii Kai Catamarans (Pier 8, street level, Honolulu 96813, tel. 808/522-7822). Patterned after an ancient Polynesian vessel, the huge *Alii Kai* catamaran casts off from historic Aloha Tower with 1,000 passengers. The deluxe dinner cruise features two open bars, a huge dinner, and an authentic Polynesian show full of colorful hulas and upbeat music. The food is good, the after-dinner show loud and fun, and everyone dances to the Alii Kai musicians on the way back to shore.

Hawaiian Cruises' Sunset Dinner Sail (343 Hobron Ln., Honolulu 96815, tel. 808/947-9971). A full Polynesian revue breaks out on the high seas on board this 110-foot vessel, which holds 550 passengers. There's an open bar followed by a sit-down dinner.

Hilton Hawaiian Village Cruise (2005 Kalia Rd., Honolulu 96815, tel. 808/949-4321). With fewer than 150 passengers, this is a more intimate cruise than the others. The boat has distinctive rainbow sails. A two-hour champagne breakfast cruise is offered, as well as the twilight dinner sail.

Tradewind Charters (350 Ward Ave., Honolulu 96814, tel. 808/533-0220). This is a real sailing experience, a little more expensive and a lot more intimate than the other cruises mentioned. The sunset sail carries no more than six people. Cost: $60. Champagne and hors d'oeuvres are extra.

Windjammer Cruises (2222 Kalakaua Ave., 6th Floor, Honolulu 96814, tel. 808/922-1200). The pride of the fleet is the 1,500-passenger *Rella Mae*, done up like a clipper ship. It was once a Hudson River excursion boat in New York. Cocktails, dinner, a Polynesian revue, and dancing to a live band are all part of the package. Then you're whisked off for more fun at "Flashback," the Hula Hut show which takes you back to the legendary performers of the '50s and '60s.

Luaus

Just about everyone who comes to Hawaii goes to at least one luau. Traditionally, the luau would last for days, with feasting, sporting events, hula, and song. But at today's scaled-down and, for the most part, inauthentic version, you're as likely to find macaroni salad on the buffet as *poi* (taro paste) and big heaps of fried chicken beside the platter of *kalua* (roasted) pig. Traditional dishes that visitors actually enjoy include *laulau* (steamed bundles of ti leaves containing pork, butterfish, and taro tops), *lomilomi* salmon (massaged until tender and served with minced onions and tomatoes), and *haupia* (dessert made from coconut). As for the notorious poi, the clean, bland taste goes nicely with something salty, like bacon or kalua pig.

If you want authenticity, look in the newspaper to see if a church or civic club is holding a luau fund-raiser. You'll not only be welcome, you'll experience some down-home Hawaiiana. One luau that can be recommended as the real thing is **Hanohano Family Luau** (tel. 808/949–5559). During a day spent in Punaluu on Oahu's north shore, you help a family prepare a luau; go fishing; and participate in sports and games. Cost: $40 adults, $29.95 children 12–16, $19.95 children 5–11.

Here are some other good luaus that emphasize fun without giving much thought to tradition. They generally cost $30–$50 adults, $25 children. Reservations are required.

Germaine's Luau (tel. 808/941–3338). You and a herd of about a thousand other people are bused to a remote beach near the industrial area. The bus ride is actually a lot of fun, while the beach and the sunset are pleasant. The service is brisk in order to feed everyone on time, and the food is so-so, but the show is warm and friendly. The bus collects passengers from 13 different Waikiki hotels; luaus start daily at 6.

Luau on the Beach (tel. 808/395–0677). Here's a nice switch—a luau right on Waikiki Beach. It takes place in front of the Outrigger Waikiki Hotel and begins with refreshing drinks at sunset. Dinner is all-you-can-eat, followed by an entertaining Polynesian show hosted by Doug Mossman of "Hawaii Five-O" fame. Tuesdays, Fridays, and Sundays at 7.

Paradise Cove Luau (tel. 808/973–5828). Another mass-produced event for a thousand or so. Once again, a bus takes you from one of six Waikiki hotel pickup points to a remote beach beside a picturesque cove on the western side of the island. There are palms and a glorious sunset, and the pageantry is fun, even informative. The food—well, you didn't come for the food, did you? Luaus begin daily at 5:30 (doors open at 5).

Royal Luau (Royal Hawaiian Hotel, 2259 Kalakaua Ave., tel. 808/923–7311). This is a notch above the rest of the commercial luaus on Oahu, perhaps because it takes place at the wonderful pink palace. With the setting sun, Diamond Head, the Pacific Ocean, and the enjoyable entertainment, who cares if the luau isn't totally authentic? Monday at 6.

Index

Personal Itinerary

Departure   *Date*

                Time

Transportation

Arrival   *Date*   *Time*

Departure   *Date*   *Time*

Transportation

Accommodations

Arrival   *Date*   *Time*

Departure   *Date*   *Time*

Transportation

Accommodations

Arrival   *Date*   *Time*

Departure   *Date*   *Time*

Transportation

Accommodations

Personal Itinerary

Arrival *Date*   *Time*

Departure *Date*   *Time*

Transportation

Accommodations

Arrival *Date*   *Time*

Departure *Date*   *Time*

Transportation

Accommodations

Arrival *Date*   *Time*

Departure *Date*   *Time*

Transportation

Accommodations

Arrival *Date*   *Time*

Departure *Date*   *Time*

Transportation

Accommodations

Personal Itinerary

Arrival *Date*   *Time*

Departure *Date*   *Time*

Transportation

Accommodations

Arrival *Date*   *Time*

Departure *Date*   *Time*

Transportation

Accommodations

Arrival *Date*   *Time*

Departure *Date*   *Time*

Transportation

Accommodations

Arrival *Date*   *Time*

Departure *Date*   *Time*

Transportation

Accommodations

Addresses

Name

Address

Telephone

Name

Address

Telephone

Name

Address

Telephone

Name

Address

Telephone

Name

Address

Telephone

Name

Address

Telephone

Name

Address

Telephone

Name

Address

Telephone

Name

Address

Telephone

Name

Address

Telephone

Name

Address

Telephone

Name

Address

Telephone

Name

Address

Telephone

Name

Address

Telephone

Name

Address

Telephone

Name

Address

Telephone

Fodor's Travel Guides

U.S. Guides

Alaska
Arizona
Boston
California
Cape Cod
The Carolinas & the
  Georgia Coast
The Chesapeake
  Region
Chicago
Colorado
Disney World & the
  Orlando Area
Florida
Hawaii
Las Vegas, Reno,
  Tahoe

Los Angeles
Maine, New
  Hampshire &
  Vermont
Maui
Miami & the
  Keys
National Parks
  of the West
New England
New Mexico
New Orleans
New York City
New York City
  (Pocket Guide)
Norway
Pacific North Coast

Philadelphia & the
  Pennsylvania
  Dutch Country
Puerto Rico
  (Pocket Guide)
The Rockies
San Diego
San Francisco
San Francisco
  (Pocket Guide)
The South
Santa, Fe Taos,
  Albuquerque
Seattle &
  Vancouver
Texas
USA

The U. S. & British
  Virgin Islands
The Upper Great
  Lakes Region
Vacations in
  New York State
Vacations on the
  Jersey Shore
Virginia & Maryland
Waikiki
Washington, D.C.

Foreign Guides

Acapulco
Amsterdam
Australia
Austria
The Bahamas
The Bahamas
  (Pocket Guide)
Baja & Mexico's Pacific
  Coast Resorts
Barbados
Barcelona, Madrid,
  Seville
Belgium &
  Luxembourg
Berlin
Bermuda
Brazil
Budapest
Budget Europe
Canada
Canada's Atlantic
  Provinces

Cancun, Cozumel,
  Yucatan Peninsula
Caribbean
Central America
China
Eastern Europe
Egypt
Europe
Europe's Great Cities
France
Germany
Great Britain
Greece
The Himalayan
  Countries
Holland
Hong Kong
India
Ireland
Israel
Italy
Italy 's Great Cities

Jamaica
Japan
Kenya, Tanzania,
  Seychelles
Korea
London
London
  (Pocket Guide)
London Companion
Mexico
Mexico City
Montreal &
  Quebec City
Morocco
New Zealand
Nova Scotia,
  New Brunswick,
  Prince Edward
  Island
Paris
Paris (Pocket Guide)
Portugal

Prague
Rio
Rome
Scandinavia
Scandinavian Cities
Scotland
Singapore
South America
South Pacific
Southeast Asia
Soviet Union
Spain
Sweden
Switzerland
Sydney
Thailand
Tokyo
Toronto
Turkey
Vienna
Yugoslavia

Wall Street Journal Guides to Business Travel

Europe
International Cities
Pacific Rim
USA & Canada

Special-Interest Guides

Bed & Breakfasts and
  Country Inns:
  Mid-Atlantic Region
Bed & Breakfasts and
  Country Inns:
  New England

Cruises and Ports
  of Call
Healthy Escapes
Fodor's Flashmaps
  New York

Fodor's Flashmaps
  Washington, D.C.
Shopping in Europe
Skiing in the U.S. &
  Canada

Smart Shopper's
  Guide to London
Sunday in New York
Touring Europe